The Compassionate Universe

The
COMPASSIONATE
UNIVERSE

EKNATH EASWARAN

Nilgiri Press

©1989 by the Blue Mountain Center of Meditation
All rights reserved. Printed in the United States of America
Designed, printed, and bound by Nilgiri Press
ISBN: *cloth, 0–915132–59–1; paper, 0–915132–58–3*
Third printing August 1995
The Blue Mountain Center of Meditation, founded in Berkeley
in 1960 by Eknath Easwaran, publishes books on how to lead the
spiritual life in the home and the community.
For information please write to
Nilgiri Press, Box 256, Tomales, California 94971.

The paper used in this book meets the minimum requirements
of American National Standard for Information Services – Permanence
of Paper for Printed Library Materials, ANSI Z39.48–1984.

Library of Congress Cataloging–in–Publication Data
will be found on the last page of this book.

Table of Contents

Part One / The Compassionate Universe

*The hypothesis of a compassionate universe
is not new, nor is the investigation I am
proposing. It has been suggested before,
at many times, in many places, and by
many great and eloquent voices. What
is different now is our unprecedented
opportunity to test it in every aspect of
life. Indeed, as the only creatures on earth
who have the power – and, it sometimes
seems, the inclination – to bring life on this
planet to an end, it is our responsibility to
test the hypothesis as it has never been
tested before.*

Chapter One

A New Era

No man is an island, entire of itself; every man is a piece of the continent, a part of the main.   – John Donne

I will never forget the day I came home from school and told my grandmother what I had learned in geography class. In our small South Indian village, my grandmother was deeply respected and loved. I could not imagine anyone wiser, yet she had never been to school or learned to read, or even traveled more than a few miles from our village. So when she met me at the gate, as she did every day, and asked me what I had learned in school, I was a bit hesitant to tell her the subject of the day's lesson. Apparently it was something every schoolboy should know and accept without difficulty. To me it was a catastrophe.

"Granny," I began with considerable agitation, "scientists have discovered that our village is nothing but an anthill compared with the sun." As always, she listened carefully to everything I had to say. I told her about the vastness of outer space, the tremendous distances between planets, and the terrible smallness of the world that had up to then been my universe: our village, the nearby forest, the Blue Mountain on the horizon. "My teacher says we are just insignificant specks in the universe, Granny. We don't matter at all."

Generally, my grandmother spoke very little, but her presence communicated a tremendous security. She said nothing now. Calmly, she opened the gate, put her hand on my shoulder, and walked inside with me.

We sat down, and it was a while before she spoke. "No one is insignificant, son," she said finally. "Have you ever looked at Hasti's eyes?" Hasti was one of the elephants that frequently served in our religious ceremonies and that I had been learning to ride. Hasti's eyes, like the eyes of all elephants, were tiny – ridiculously small, really, for an animal so huge. "She has no idea how big she is," Granny said, "because she looks out at the world through such tiny eyes."

At the time, Granny's words went right over my head. It was not until much later, after many years and much seeking and questioning, that I began to understand why she answered me the way she did – and why she lived the way she did. That search, and the understanding I eventually reached, are the subject of this book. I have come to believe that her answer, and the comprehensive vision of human nature it was based on, have a great deal to offer the world at this critical period in history, as it becomes clear that our present way of life is endangering not only our own health and well-being but that of the earth itself.

My grandmother lived in a universe filled with life. It was impossible for her to conceive of any creature – even the smallest insect, let alone a human being – as insignificant. In every leaf, flower, animal, and star she saw the expression of a compassionate universe, whose laws were not competition and survival of the fittest but cooperation, artistry, and thrift.

Not that she talked about any of this; it was simply the way she lived and thought. Indeed, few of us in that small South Indian village could even have begun to express this idea verbally. None of us lived up to the example my grandmother set, but we all trusted and looked up to her. In our way of life, our farming, our business and barter, our friendships, we were guided by her ideal of an individual life rooted in continuous harmony with life as a whole.

In every aspect, life in our village was very close. Our lives had been woven together through centuries of depending on each other. If my mother wanted a new pot, she would send for the village potter, whose family had been making pots for my family for centuries, and he would turn out just what she wanted. If my cousins needed new jewelry, they would call on the village goldsmith, who would come and fashion earrings for them right on the veranda of our house, just as his father and grandfather had done.

We traveled little, since everything we needed was right there in the village. I received my elementary school education, for instance, on the veranda of our ancestral home. Our homes were built of bricks made in the village and teak from the nearby forest, and for entertainment we were often visited by some of the finest South Indian classical dance, music, and drama troupes.

Agriculturally as well, we were self-sufficient. Our crop yields were not astonishing, but they were substantial, and for centuries our traditional method of farming, based on the rhythms of nature, natural pest control, and natural fertilizers, had enriched the soil. Following Granny's example, we tried to treat every part of nature with love and respect. The earth was our home, she would have said, but no less was it home to the oxen that pulled our plows or the elephants that roamed in the forest and worked for us. They lived with us as partners whose well-being was inseparable from our own.

But I think it was in times of mourning and celebration that we understood just how deeply our lives were intertwined. A death or birth in any family touched us almost as deeply as if it affected our own kin. Much later, when I came to read John Donne, I recognized the life of our village in his lines: "No man is an island, entire of itself; every man is a piece of the continent, a part of the main; if a clod be washed away by the sea, Europe is the less, as well as if a promontory were, as well as if a manor of thy friends or of thine own were; any man's death diminishes me, because I am involved in mankind; and therefore never send to know for whom the bell tolls; it tolls for thee."

Because of these enduring bonds, we had no need for some of the impersonal institutions that have become essential in industrial society, like life insurance and social security. Instead we had families and friends who were ready to help in any circumstance. Within such an atmosphere, there was little or no crime; in fact, I never even saw a policeman until I went away to college.

Of course, we did not live in an ideal world. In a prosperous village like ours there was little poverty, but diseases like cholera and smallpox were not uncommon. It is not that no one was ever hurt, or that people never quarreled or manipulated each other; but when such things happened, we knew quite clearly that they were discordant, that they did not fit in with the way life should be. It was not an ideal world, but it was a world with an ideal.

My grandmother embodied this ideal, and the depth of her commitment to it helped all of us to find it in ourselves. Cooperation, artistry, thrift, and compassion: my grandmother saw these laws at work everywhere, and they were the foundation of everything she did. That is why my geography teacher's comment must have seemed a little ridiculous to her. Our significance as human beings was not a philosophical issue or a matter for intellectual debate. It was a daily, continuous experience, more real than anything else.

You might think my grandmother lived in a state of blessed innocence, untouched by the world's problems. True, she did not read newspapers, and she knew nothing about physics or chemistry, but in the give-and-take of daily life she showed a wisdom and loving authority that never altered, even when she was faced with severe trials. I remember her sitting for days nursing cholera victims, whom all the other villagers were afraid to come near, without a trace of fear or despair, always secure in her compassion. And many times she kept the traditional all-night vigil with the body of a relative who had just died – a tremendous act of love for the rest of us, who wanted the vigil kept but were afraid to set foot in the room reserved for the corpse.

I trusted and loved my grandmother, and my ancestral family, but by the time I finished high school it was hard not to feel the pull of a different way of life – one that was already making changes in our village and traditional attitudes. As one of my teachers said, repeating what he had heard in Madras, if India were to survive, we would have to unlearn all our village ways and adopt the new technological methods of agriculture and production. Words like these came with the imprimatur of a dazzling world, a world of high ambitions and extraordinary technical achievements – a world I was curious to see and explore for myself.

When I was sixteen, my grandmother, who had always warmly encouraged my education, sent me off to college. There I was able to follow my passionate love for English literature. Before me opened the rich world of Shakespeare, Wordsworth, Shelley, and Coleridge, of Dickens and George Bernard Shaw. Before long I was sporting a blue blazer and falling completely under the spell of Western society, with its sophistication, its scientific brilliance, its literary and artistic genius. Eventually, I embarked on a relatively promising career as public speaker, writer, and professor of English literature.

I was not alone. At the time, a heady feeling of possibility inspired the discussions of scientists, engineers, philosophers, and writers all over India. Sensing the tremendous power of the scientific method, and inspired by the promise of a life free from superstition and unnecessary suffering, some of the best minds of our generation joined the search for the forces that rule nature and for the power to direct those forces. The successes were tremendous. For a while, it seemed that even the concept of impossibility had stepped aside. Cars, airplanes, and radios became commonplace. Astronomers probed the vastness of outer space as new galaxies swam into view. Physicists split the atom.

Personally, I found the world of letters fascinating and challenging. I spent several years teaching at a major Indian university, greatly enjoying my contact with students. I was engaged in a career that seemed adapted best to my intellectual capacities and emotional needs – the sharing of great literature with young men and women who were deeply responsive to my presentation. I was also coming to be known in the world of Indian letters, and I was quite certain this was the direction that would take me to complete fulfillment. My only pressing concerns were scholarly questions: Where did Shakespeare get the material for Hamlet? Or, what were the influences that molded Shaw's early plays?

Midway through life, however, at about the time when my gray hairs were beginning to outnumber the black, these questions began to be replaced by others I had never before taken seriously but that every mature person needs to answer in some way: Why am I here? What is the purpose of my life? Is there nothing I can do to escape the emptiness of death?

Around me, in the cities and villages of India, millions of people did not have enough to eat and were struggling to survive without proper clothing or shelter. This was a clear and obvious hunger. There were many things about the world I would have liked to change, and in my own small way I felt I was helping to change them. But I had not expected that, in literature and the world of the university, in a society just beginning to enjoy the comforts of the modern industrial era, I would have experienced a gnawing hunger that would not let me rest.

I read widely in literature, psychology, and science, looking for answers to the questions that had suddenly become so urgent. But after years of reading, of going to lectures and plays and concerts, I came out, to paraphrase Omar Khayyám, by the same door I went in.

For all the apparent success of modern industrial society, the answers it provides to these questions are at best inadequate. When we ask what the purpose of our lives is, we are told: to have more things, to experience more sensations, to have fun, to become rich or powerful or famous. I looked at the lives of the men and women who led the world in literature, art, music, dance, politics, and science. I had admired these people since my freshman days, yet now I found that although they had sometimes achieved great things, their lives did not shine. They had not found a way to live without despair or depression. Some of the most famous had even judged life not worth living, while others found themselves in that most terrible of conditions, utter loneliness. Success had proved to be no shield against the ups and downs of life. Nowhere did I find anyone like my grandmother: secure under all circumstances, unselfish, wise.

In the literature I was reading and teaching, great voices spoke of an emptiness at the center of life. Life is a desert, wrote Thomas Hardy, except for one or two oases. We live, wrote Matthew Arnold, "on a darkling plain . . . where ignorant armies clash by night." From science, the answer was no different. The discoveries of modern physics and biology were generally interpreted as proving that the universe is a meaningless play of energy and matter onto which we project our desire for something of lasting value. Even our deepest hopes and dreams, according to the influential mathematician and philosopher Bertrand Russell, were "nearly certain" to be proved "the outcome of accidental collocations of atoms. . . . Brief and powerless is man's life," he wrote; "on him and all his race the slow, sure doom falls pitiless and dark. Blind to good and evil, reckless of destruction, omnipotent matter rolls on its relentless course."

Ideals, fulfillment, love: according to the industrial world, these inner experiences were accidents or fantasies. Mother Earth – the mother who cared for and fed us as I was growing up – was only a mass of organic and inorganic matter to which we had attached a certain emotional value. Vayu, the god of air, Varuna, the god of water, whom we worshiped by keeping our air and water pure and clean: these were old superstitions to be cast aside, along with the loving care that went with them.

In boardrooms and halls of power, the mood was optimistic – and opportunistic. There were more than enough trees, more than enough oil, clean water, and fresh air. The restraints imposed by the old poetic, religious images were simply holding back the progress that would eventually bring prosperity to the entire world. To the industrial eye, my grandmother's compassionate universe did not exist; it was a figment of our village imagination. Such an idea had possessed a certain survival value before the advent of technology. Now, though, it could be dispensed with and replaced with ever more powerful ways of satisfying our desires.

Yet somehow I felt that a human being needs to fit, to be an intimately connected, deeply involved part of the world. The beauty of nature, the experience of love – were these things mere superstitions, our own projections onto an indifferent or even hostile Nature? So far as the industrial

world was concerned, something in me was hopelessly out
of date. I just could not feel at ease with what it seemed to
be telling me: each of us is a separate, competing speck in a
meaningless universe. If you are lucky, you are a happy
speck, with a prestigious speck of a job in a prosperous
speck of a country. If not, you are an unhappy speck and
should try to acquire what it takes to become a happy one.

Clearly, I could not go back to my childhood. The world
was changing quickly, and I could see that soon there would
be no place to hide from this conflict. But neither could
I wholly accept the world that was replacing the compassionate universe I had grown up in. True, the industrial
era had brought us some great material advantages, and
many of its medical and engineering advances had helped relieve suffering; but it was, in the end, a world of the bottom
line, concerned not with people but with profit. In India and
around the world, it was voraciously swallowing up the old
ways of living and thinking, of farming and doing business,
and replacing them with new ones that had little place for the
individual, or the environment, or future generations.

Even then a few farsighted observers warned that the environment would suffer, although no one quite predicted
the reports we hear now from ecologists, marine biologists,
and atmospheric scientists. At the same time, I was beginning to sense that there was nothing in the industrial world's
endless whirl of new products and pleasures that would
compensate for the things receding ever farther into the dis-
tance: our hope for a peaceful world; the knowledge that
our children will inherit a healthy earth; the feeling of
having a high purpose; the experience of being a blessing
instead of a curse on the rest of life.

At about that time, like many young Indians, I began to

develop a passionate interest in Mahatma Gandhi. By the 1930s, of course, Gandhi had become the most influential leader of India's independence movement and a world-famous political figure. But to me, and to many of the people of India – especially the students – he was much more. Every day he received piles of letters from the many Indians who regarded him as *Bapu,* "Father," and none went unanswered – even if he had to stay up all night writing.

He wrote on every conceivable topic, from the philosophy of nonviolence to race relations, from homespun cloth to vegetarianism. There seemed no limit to his curiosity, or his daring, or his devotion to serving others. Every Monday, when I received his journal *Harijan,* I would devour his latest article or published letter from start to finish. Everything about Gandhi's life fascinated me, but I was particularly eager to learn more about his transformation from a fearful, unsuccessful lawyer into a leader who, without any material resources or technological prowess, had stood the industrial era on its head.

To me, it was the riddle of the century. The British Empire – with no lack of firepower, factories, or technology – was the quintessential world power of the industrial era, and it had used ruthless ingenuity for several centuries to keep a great part of the world subject. Yet, in its struggle to subdue India, it was proving to be no match for the man who was then living in Sevagram, "the village of service," which he had founded on the sweltering plains of central India. The greatest empire the world had ever seen was being brought to its knees by a "little brown man in a loincloth."

Gandhi's campaigns, and indeed his life, seemed far more than just a struggle for independence. His success was marking the end of an era – not just for the British Empire but for an entire phase of our civilization. A new era was beginning, and I wanted to meet the man who had started it.

The Power of Salt

*As human beings, our greatness lies not so
much in being able to remake the world –
that is the myth of the 'atomic age' – as in
being able to remake ourselves.*

      – *Mahatma Gandhi*

I got off the train at Wardha, walked a few miles along a dusty country road, and reached Sevagram about five o'clock in the afternoon. There I found a small crowd of young men and women waiting in front of Gandhiji's cottage. They told me Gandhi had been at work since early morning, with only a short lunch break. As we waited, I tried to picture him to myself. He would be gaunt, I imagined, from hard work and an austere diet; perhaps he would stoop a little, bearing the weight of a subcontinent on his shoulders; and after a long day of meetings, he would be tired and irritable. He probably would want nothing to do with us.

The bamboo door opened. With the springy step of a teenager and with a vivacious twinkle in his eyes, Gandhi emerged and strode off for his evening walk, beckoning – to me particularly, it seemed, although there were several others – for us to walk with him. I was a pretty good walker, and less than half his age, but I could hardly keep up with him. It was like trying to keep pace with a sand-piper.

I was entranced. How was it possible? Gandhi seemed profoundly relaxed. Everything about him radiated vigor, peace, and boundless energy. How could anyone withstand that kind of pressure with so much grace? How could any-one witness as much suffering as he did, care so deeply about it, and work fifteen hours a day to relieve it, yet still be filled with such infectious good humor?

At Sevagram I found myself among young people from around the world – Americans, Japanese, Africans, Europeans, even Britons – who had come to see Gandhi and to help in his work. Whether a person's skin was white, brown, or black, whether he or she supported or opposed him, seemed to make no difference to Gandhi: he related to all with ease and respect. Almost immediately, he made us feel we were part of his own family.

Indeed, I think that, in a private corner of our hearts, we all saw ourselves in him. I did. It was as if a precious element common to all of us had been extracted and purified to shine forth brightly as the Mahatma, the Great Soul. That very commonness was what moved us most – the feeling that in spite of all our fears and resentments and petty faults we too were made of such stuff. The Great Soul was our soul.

At that time, of course, there were many observers who said Gandhi was extraordinary, an exception to the limitations that hold back the rest of the human race. Others dismissed him – some with great respect, others with less – as just another great man who was leaving his mark on history. Yet, according to him, there was no one more ordinary. "I claim to be an average man of less than average ability," he often repeated. "I have not the shadow of a doubt that any man or woman can achieve what I have, if he or she would make the same effort and cultivate the same hope and faith."

The fact is, while most people think of ordinariness as a fault or limitation, Gandhi had discovered in it the very meaning of life – and of history. For him, it was not the famous or the rich or the powerful who would change the course of history. If the future is to differ from the past, he taught, if we are to leave a peaceful and healthy earth for our children, it will be the ordinary man and woman who do it: not by becoming extraordinary, but by discovering that our greatest strength lies not in how much we differ from each other but in how much – how very much – we are the same.

This faith in the power of the individual formed the foundation for Gandhi's extremely compassionate view of the industrial era's large-scale problems, as well as of the smaller but no less urgent troubles we found in our own lives. Our problems, he would say, are not inevitable; they are not, as some historians and biologists have suggested, a necessary side effect of civilization.

On the contrary, war, economic injustice, and pollution arise because we have not yet learned to make use of our most civilizing capacities: the creativity and wisdom we all have as our birthright. When even one person comes into full possession of these capacities, our problems are shown in their true light: they are simply the results of avoidable – though deadly – errors of judgment.

Gandhi formulated a series of diagnoses of the twentieth century's seemingly perpetual state of crisis, which he called "the seven social sins." I prefer to think of them as seven social ailments, since the problems they address are not crimes calling for punishment but crippling diseases that are punishment enough in themselves. These seven diagnoses cover every area of modern life, and volumes could be written about each of them. Here, though, I will be paying particular attention to the way they affect our relationship with the environment.

Perhaps the most compassionate of all seven is the one I will treat first, *knowledge without character,* which traces all our difficulties to a simple lack of connection between what we know is good for us and our ability to act on that knowledge. Then there is *science without humanity* – referring to the experiment we are conducting on ourselves and our planet, based on the absurd hypothesis that production, consumption, and national boundaries are more important than people or the earth.

Wealth without work points out the greatest failing of our society: it offers our young people no ideal or goal worthy of their ambition. Without a focus for their tremendous energy and talent, more and more of our brightest, most promising young people are turning to drugs or a life of sterile moneymaking, just at the time when the world needs their idealism most. Then there is *commerce without morality,* the business equivalent of science without humanity: a frenzy of economic activity based not on human need or the needs of the environment, but on an unexamined addiction to profit.

The last three diagnoses thrust us directly into the most challenging problems of the coming decades. *Politics without principles* refers to politics, from the governmental to the personal level, based on an almost total lack of faith in human nature, while *pleasure without conscience* concerns the destructive life-style based on that lack of faith. Finally, *worship without self-sacrifice* suggests that we have overlooked our most precious evolutionary resources: our idealism, our sensitivity to the suffering of others, and our sense of unity with the life around us.

To me, Gandhi's list is one of the best X rays of contemporary society ever taken. In this book I will use these seven diagnoses as starting points for a practical discussion of how we can support the world's transition into a healthy, peaceful postindustrial era – a transition already taking place in the lives of many thoughtful people around the world. What I am presenting is not a theory but simply the results of my own experience. I have become convinced that it is possible, while retaining all the beneficial contributions of the industrial era, gradually to replace competition and the profit motive with active, modern applications of the laws of a compassionate universe: cooperation, artistry, and thrift.

What may not be clear in Gandhi's list, but what shines through to anyone who knows something of his life, is that this is no gloomy prediction of catastrophe; it is a positive statement of hope. A less bold physician might have pronounced the case too far gone: "Perhaps if you had come to me sooner . . . "

Gandhi says, "It's not too late at all. You just don't yet know what you are capable of." Behind his list is the daring implication that the solution to our problems does not have to be invented. It is already here. People do not have to become something they are not; they need to learn who and what they really are.

It may be difficult to have faith in the vision of the human being and the hope for world peace and health these diagnoses are based on. At this point in history, it is sometimes difficult even to imagine politics based on honesty and cooperation, or world commerce based on mutual respect and care – let alone believe they are possible.

Indeed, many have regarded Gandhi as too idealistic. Yet I think he saw more clearly than most of us that the industrial world is a very rough place. Politics without principles, commerce without morality, pleasure without conscience – these are unsparing, incisive diagnoses. I would suggest that it is only because Gandhi had an inexhaustible faith in human nature – based not on philosophy but on his own personal experience in leading a troubled nation of four hundred million people – that he could see human failings so clearly.

"As human beings," he once wrote, "our greatness lies not so much in being able to remake the world – that is the myth of the 'atomic age' – as in being able to remake ourselves." Had these words appeared as part of a social theory or an essay in theology, perhaps we could dismiss them as overly optimistic or moralizing. But they come from a man who, without firing a single shot, changed the face of modern Asia and the world – all by remaking himself. During the twenty years he spent in South Africa, Gandhi remade his entire character, transforming himself from a timid lawyer who could barely stammer out the facts of a case into one of the most courageous and effective leaders the world has seen. In situations in which other leaders would have alienated rivals or succumbed to animosity, Gandhi won over his opponents with perseverance, good humor, and love. However unlikely it seemed, Gandhi's perspective worked. He had remade himself, and having done so, he offered the world a hope-filled alternative to war, pollution, and exploitation.

Knowledge Without Character

To me, the central paradox of the twentieth century is that despite our powerful intellectual skills and our ingenious engineering and medical achievements, we still lack the ability to live wisely. We send sophisticated satellites into space that beam us startling information about the destruction of the environment, yet we do little, if anything, to stop that destruction. The countries of the world spend nearly a trillion dollars a year on weapons and military forces, and are planning to spend even more, while twenty million Americans – twelve million of them children – go hungry, and forty thousand babies in Third World countries die of hunger or hunger-related causes every day.

As Martin Luther King, Jr., put it, we live in a world of "guided missiles and misguided men," where few technical problems are too complex to solve but we find it impossible to cope with the most basic of life's challenges: how to live together in peace and health. In our lucid moments we see that we are doing great harm to ourselves and our planet, but somehow, for all our intellectual understanding, we cannot seem to change the way we think and live.

Yet the problem is not in our intellect. In itself, the intellect is neither good nor bad. Nevertheless, as the twentieth century has shown us again and again, it can be an expert at both. It can as easily design hydrogen bombs as build hospitals, invent napalm as discover penicillin. Like a genie, it makes a good servant if we are its masters, but we are not always its masters.

This is not to say we are bad people. The problem is simply that we have not yet completed our education. When Gandhi speaks of knowledge without character, he is not implying that we know too much for our own good. He is saying that because we do not understand what our real needs are, we are unable to use our tremendous technical expertise in a way that might make our lives more secure and fulfilling. Instead, we treat every problem as if it were a matter for technology, or chemistry, or economics, even when it has nothing to do with these things.

Every day, for example, dozens of new products appear, promising to satisfy our deepest desires. We are barraged with messages – subliminal and otherwise – on billboards and in magazines, on television and in the movies, telling us that everything we are looking for in life can be found in a car or a bowl of ice cream or a cigarette.

Although we may not consciously see these messages' effect on our lives, it is real. Indeed, the advertising industry has become quite scientific in learning how we respond to it. "Over the last five years," one advertising executive said in an article I read recently, "advertisers have been strategically trying to elicit an emotional response. You don't just focus on features but on establishing a personality, building an emotional aura that will appeal to a certain person."

The reason all this research is necessary, of course, is that most of these advertisements are trying to sell us things we do not need. "Demand," says another executive, "is created by advertising." The article goes on to explain this trend: "For a large segment of the U.S. population, basic physical needs have been met. Products must now be sold, say some advertisers, on the basis of meeting some unfulfilled psychological need." As one observer remarked, "The feeling a man gets from being a Marlboro man is often more important than from smoking Marlboro cigarettes."

The hidden message is that what we own or eat or smoke has the power to endow us with self-respect. Actually, I would say it is the other way around. Your car may be useful and comfortable, it may have a wet bar and a cellular phone, but that is not why it is dignified. You, a human being, are the one who gives dignity to your car by driving it. If it were not for you, that car would be only a hunk of metal. Similarly with other things: *you* give luster to the diamond you wear and fragrance to your perfume.

I recall my grandmother bringing this spirit to every aspect of her life – and her example set the tone for our village. She was a deeply independent woman who refused to let any material possession interfere with that independence. The way she saw it, when we depend on possessions for dignity or fulfillment, we are giving away part of our freedom. We become servants to the things we bought to serve us.

My uncle, who taught English at our village school, once made this point to us with characteristic flair. He wrote on the blackboard "John owns a Ford car," then asked us to write the same sentence in the passive voice. We all wrote "A Ford car is owned by John." All, that is, except one fellow in the back, who had written "A Ford car owns John."

We started to laugh, but my uncle held up his hand. "The

rest of you may know grammar," he said, "but this young man knows life."

Several decades later, when I first came to the United States, I was surprised to hear a young American say the same thing. "That man doesn't own his car," he said as one of his friends roared by in a Thunderbird. "It owns him. He's got to work six days a week and take on extra jobs to pay for it."

As we enter the last decade of the twentieth century, can't the same thing almost be said of us? Over the past fifty years, the automobile, like so many of our appliances and machines, has sped down the now-familiar psychological highway from desirable luxury to basic necessity to tyrannical master. We no longer choose to drive a car – we have to: there are so many things to do, so little time to do them, and so far to travel in between. We rush about from place to place, caught in a perilous game of catch-up, and the price is high: nearly fifty thousand Americans lose their lives in traffic accidents every year. The irony is, we are often in such a hurry that we can't get anywhere. I have read that commute time in Tokyo and London now is often less by bicycle than by car; and to judge by rush hour on our freeways, our situation is not much different.

Worse than the loss of time, of course, is the threat to our health. In each of those cars, according to recent research conducted in Los Angeles, commuters are exposed to two to four times the levels of cancer-causing toxic chemicals found outdoors. And as it idles there on the freeway, the average American car makes a significant contribution to the greenhouse effect, pumping its own weight in carbon into the atmosphere each year.

These things are not secrets. We have all heard them many times before, but we find it hard to do anything about them. Our cities and towns have grown in such a way that we feel helpless without a car. And as our cities expand ever farther into the surrounding countryside, the situation promises to get even worse.

The problem is that the roots of our dependence on the auto go deeper than the desire for a convenient mode of transportation. There is a much more powerful force at work here – a force that characterizes almost every activity in industrial society: profit. Under the relentless domination of the profit motive, we have remade our country in the image of the automobile. As the political historian Richard Barnet writes, describing America in the middle decades of this century,

> Buying highways meant buying motels, quick food eateries, . . . and the culture of suburbia. . . . The highway system was the nation's only physical plan, and more than anything else it determined the appearance of cities and the stretches in between. In choosing the automobile as the engine of growth, the highway and automotive planners scrapped mass transit.

Several corporations went so far as to buy existing trolley and train systems, tear them up, and replace them with buses they manufactured, burning gas they sold, and rolling on tires they made. This happened with more than one hundred electric railway systems in forty-five cities.

Oil shortages and higher gasoline prices have led us to regret turning a blind eye toward such practices, yet we go on driving more and more, drilling new oil wells, making and buying more and bigger cars. In just one hundred years, urged on by the profit motive and the media conditioning that driving is entertainment and our car is an extension of our personality, we have used up nearly half of the world's known petroleum reserves, fouled our air, and put our oceans and beaches at continual risk from oil spills.

Now, I have nothing against automobiles. I have a car,

and I appreciate its utility. All I would say is, it is important to remember who is serving whom. If we were the
masters of our machines – and our lives – we *would* have
good, well-made cars and good roads on which to drive,
but wouldn't we also use them sparingly, so our children
and our children's children would have enough oil left to
enjoy a trip through the countryside? Wouldn't we carpool and use mass transit whenever possible so the air they
breathe would be clean and health-giving? Wouldn't we reduce our demand for oil and take great care with the oil we
do use, so the beaches they visit would be clean, with spar-
kling sand and healthy birds and seals playing in the waves?

Nor am I suggesting that there is anything wrong in a
businessperson making enough profit to support his or her
family in comfort – everyone should have this opportunity.
But in the industrial era we have exaggerated the importance of profit out of all proportion to its natural place in
business. We have become addicted to it, and that is a very
dangerous situation.

Most addictions begin innocently enough. "Just one
more helping, one more bowl of ice cream, one more cigarette, one more drink for the road." That is how it starts –
just one more: "Let's sell just one more new car, make one
more dollar, pump one more gallon of gas."

When we give in to that desire repeatedly, with a second
helping, a second smoke, a second drink, or a second sniff,
it becomes a habit – not just one more but one every day:
"The stockholders want to see this quarter's profits rising
above last quarter's. Get the general manager on the phone
and tell him to increase production, bolster demand, and
heat up consumption. And do it yesterday."

With a habit we still have a choice whether to give in or
not, but when a habit continues long enough, we lose our
power to choose. Our feeling of security becomes so closely

attached to the thing we crave that we must have it, whatever the cost. The habit has become a compulsion, and we have become its servant. We will do anything for a profit, even if it means sacrificing our children's precious seas, air, and earth. "Round-the-clock cleanup crews for oil tankers? No, we can save a few thousand dollars. Air pollution controls? No, that would cut into our profits."

This is what Gandhi means by knowledge without character – a lack of connection between what we know to be in everyone's long-range best interest and our ability to act on that knowledge. It has become the cornerstone of much of our business and our lives. Consider this plea for "forced consumption," made by a marketing consultant in the mid-1950s, as he outlines the course for the following three and a half decades: "Our enormously productive economy . . . demands that we make consumption a way of life, that we convert the buying and use of goods into rituals, that we seek our spiritual satisfactions in consumption. . . . We need things consumed, burned up, worn out, replaced, and discarded at an ever-growing rate." That consultant was not alone. Since then, many government and industry leaders have called on us to make consumption a way of life. To a great extent, we have complied.

The Colonization

Anyone who has tried to overcome a powerful addiction like smoking or drinking or overeating knows there can be a broad, dangerous chasm between what we know is good for us and our ability to act on it. Once a habit has been conditioning the nervous system for many years, beating a path to the refrigerator or the cigarette machine or the lotto counter, it has also carved a track far below the conscious level of the mind, in the hidden world of the unconscious.

When an addiction has established itself like this in the unconscious, it can have a devastating effect on behavior. No matter how much we are told about the dangers, we often find ourselves falling helplessly back into old habits. Once, while waiting for a friend at the hospital, I saw a paralyzed man in a wheelchair struggle for some time with a package of cigarettes. Despite the fact that he could hardly move, a powerful compulsion was telling him to get out a cigarette, lift it to his lips, and light it. Laboriously and painfully, he complied. It took him nearly a quarter of an hour.

Now consider another patient.

Few people realize that many of the food items now sold in a typical American supermarket – from potato chips to tomatoes to frozen pizzas – need an injection of petroleum at every step of their production and marketing. Herbicide, fertilizer, insecticide, tractor fuel, processing fuel, plastic packaging, transportation to the supermarket, refrigeration: all these require fossil fuels in some form – usually petroleum. Why use all this oil, when we have managed to do quite well for millennia with only sun, water, and soil? As I understand it, the answer begins with a seed: not just any seed, but a seed created after years of research and development.

Farmers and food processors have begun using seeds produced by sophisticated hybridization techniques and genetic engineering to grow fruit or vegetable to meet shipping and processing needs, like a potato that makes a perfect potato chip or french fry, or a tomato with the best shape, skin, and consistency for canning. The only financial drawback to such seeds is that they require a host of petroleum and chemical products to achieve the high yields they promise. Ingeniously, many firms have overcome that drawback by acquiring their own chemical, petroleum, and farm equipment companies. Some have gone so far as to acquire a genetic engineering firm that can design seeds to require just the products their companies manufacture. In this way, they can almost give away the seeds and still make a handsome profit.

From the consumer's point of view, I am afraid there are other drawbacks. Most of the tomatoes grown today are bred for profit, not nutrition; these are not the juicy, delicious tomatoes, ripened on the vine, you might once have tasted in your mother's kitchen garden. They are hard, almost square hybrids, ripened on a truck and often covered with dangerous chemical residues. They are genetically engineered for high yield, attractive color, disease resistance, and ease of canning or shipping. Only after these things has taste been considered, and nutrition hardly at all.

Then why do we buy them? Why not demand something better? I would suggest that the answer is to be found not in our economics but in our mental state. We have been conditioned to look to food for our inner fulfillment. Food can entertain us, we are told. It is exciting; it is romantic; it is adventurous; it is dignified. Vast sums of money are spent trying to get us to buy a certain brand of potato chip or to prefer one brand of frozen pizza over another. In the midst of this carnival atmosphere, it is easy to forget that the real purpose of food is to nourish our bodies.

Doctors remind us frequently of the consequences – junk food and heart disease, pesticides and cancer – but health is not just a matter between us and our physician. The health effects of industrial agriculture go far beyond what happens to us when we eat its products. They pose an even greater risk to the food supply our children will depend on in coming decades.

"Like it or not," the president of a major agricultural corporation declared in 1984, "food production has been transformed from a local operation into an international business
dependent on high technology." In other words, agriculture
has become agribusiness, and that means agriculture dependent on petroleum and chemical products. Between 1950
and 1979, according to the Worldwatch Institute's 1988 *State
of the World* report, farmers increased petroleum use at least
fivefold.

Consider the many different ways petrochemical products are used in producing a bag of agribusiness corn
chips. First, because agribusiness farms are usually very
large, a vast amount of petroleum is needed to run all the
machines that plow and fertilize the field, that plant, spray,
and harvest the corn, and then process, package, and ship it.

But that is only the machinery. Contemporary hybrid
seeds are designed to produce greater yields than ordinary
seeds, but they work best only when used with high-
nutrient artificial fertilizers, manufactured in a chemical
factory, using petroleum as an ingredient and as a processing fuel. Then, to control insects, large quantities of
powerful insecticides are used – introducing hundreds of
toxic chemicals never before found in nature.

Now, high-nutrient chemical fertilizers nourish not only
the corn but all sorts of other plants and weeds that compete with it. At the same time, insecticides harm the birds
and insects that feed on those weeds. The sensible response
might be to use less chemical fertilizer and insecticide and to
apply them only when needed, if at all. But this kind of care
is impossible on a huge farm, where the chemicals are applied with large machinery or by airplane, hundreds of acres
per day. The profit-oriented solution is to come up with yet
another product that can be sold to every farmer who uses

chemical fertilizers: herbicides. With tremendous ingenuity, agribusiness engineers have even begun to match specific herbicides to the crop's genetic pattern so the herbicide will kill everything but the corn.

There is a hitch, though. In all this innovation, a great deal of attention is paid to the ratio of gross income to net profit, to the glamorous appearance of an ear of corn, or to the ease with which it can become a corn chip. Yet little thought is given to the topsoil, that fragile layer of minerals, organic matter, and insect life on which almost our entire food supply depends.

Although chemical fertilizers contain many of the nutrients a crop needs, they lack the humus and organic matter needed to nourish what is, after all, a living ecosystem. The topsoil's earthworms and microorganisms depend on that organic matter. So does the topsoil's capacity to hold water and prevent erosion. When chemical fertilizers are used continuously, the soil literally begins to starve. It loses its ability to retain water, and it needs ever-increasing amounts of irrigation. Then, as herbicides and insecticides are applied every season, year after year – eventually poisoning the microscopic life of the topsoil – the most important element in world agriculture is reduced to lifeless dust.

Due in part to these practices, one third of the United States' cropland is seriously affected by erosion. At the same time, more and more water is being used for irrigation, thus depleting the abundant water resources that helped make this country so prosperous. Some researchers warn that in coming decades we could see a dust bowl much more serious than the one that devastated this country in the nineteen thirties.

It does not make sense. Perhaps it might if the foods we ended up with were better – better tasting or better for our health – but they are not. It might make sense if all these chemicals and oil helped the individual farmer, or made the earth healthier, or saved precious resources. But they do not. Or it might make sense if they really did ensure the safety and abundance of our food supply. They do just the opposite.

The biologist Dr. Barry Commoner writes,

> One can almost admire the enterprise and clever salesmanship of the petrochemical industry. Somehow it has managed to convince the farmer that he should give up the free solar energy that drives the natural cycles and, instead, buy the needed energy – in the form of fertilizer and fuel – from the petrochemical industry. Not content with that commercial coup, these industrial giants have completed their conquest of the farmer by going into competition with what the farmer produces. They have introduced into the market a series of competing synthetics: synthetic fiber, which competes with cotton and wool; detergents, which compete with soap made of natural oils and fat; plastics, which compete with wood; and pesticides that compete with birds and ladybugs, which used to be free.

"The giant corporations," he concludes, "have made a colony out of rural America."

The same story is being repeated around the globe, as much in Third World countries as in developed nations. As Dr. Commoner rightly says, we see ourselves – not just this nation but the entire world – colonized. This, for me, is a terribly painful thought. I grew up in a nation that had been colonized by the British Empire, just as this country was. I have seen firsthand the devastation left when the profit motive blinds people to the consequences of their actions. Before the British took over India, Bengal was a rich, productive region. The misery of Calcutta today is a monument to greed unharnessed. Is this the kind of legacy we want to leave our children?

To Dr. Commoner's observation, however, I would make a vital addition: these corporations and advertisers are not someone else. It is not some outside nation or group that has colonized us. Petroleum-dependent agriculture may begin with a seed and the desire for profit, but it ends with us, when we reach for an item on the supermarket shelf. Without our cooperation and support, none of this would take place. We have helped in every stage of our own colonization, almost unconsciously believing that our dignity, fulfillment, and happiness are to be found in food or possessions or profits. We have become servants to our own unintended greed, and it is not a benevolent master.

The writer Thomas Berry describes it well in his book *The Dream of the Earth*. To me, this paragraph is a catalog of the effects of knowledge without character:

> We can break the mountains apart; we can drain the rivers and flood the valleys. We can turn the most luxuriant forests into throwaway paper products. We can tear apart the great grass cover of the western plains and pour toxic chemicals into the soil and pesticides onto the fields until the soil is dead and blows away in the wind. We can pollute the air with acids, the rivers with sewage, the seas with oil – all this in a kind of intoxication with our power for devastation at an order of magnitude beyond all reckoning. We can invent computers capable of processing ten million calculations per second. And why? To increase the volume and the speed with which we move natural resources through the consumer economy to the junk pile or the waste heap. Our managerial skills are measured by the competence manifested in accelerating this process. If in these activities the topography of the planet is damaged, if the environment is made inhospitable for a multitude of living species, then so be it. We are, supposedly, creating a technological wonderworld.

The entire industrial world, this technological wonder-world, has been built up because we have been watching helplessly, hypnotized by its brilliance, unable to turn our eyes away from the life of luxury it promises, or to make the small changes in our daily habits which might mitigate its destructiveness. This is knowledge without character – extraordinary technical expertise without the will or wisdom to use it well.

In Gandhi's perspective, it is up to individuals like you and me to reverse this situation. Environmental abuse and exploitation are not "necessary evils" – no evil is necessary. In fact, Gandhi went so far as to say that evil in itself is not even real; it exists only as long as we support it. The moment we withdraw our support – the moment we make the connection between what we know and how we behave – it begins to collapse. As the eighteenth century British statesman Edmund Burke put it, "The only thing necessary for the triumph of evil is for good men to do nothing."

Nevertheless, in our current situation, good men and women have little time to lose. At a breakneck pace, knowledge without character is making drastic changes in our atmosphere, our agricultural resources, our forests, and our seas. The cost in life is immeasurable, though it is the sad task of many of today's scientists and naturalists to bear witness to it. They draw up lists of the eight hundred species of higher animals now threatened – the elephant, the whale, the snow leopard, the polar bear, the jaguar, and the cheetah among them. They describe the rate of disappearance of many lesser known species, and estimate the devastation still to come. Within the next two to three decades, they say, if present rates of destruction of the world's rainforests continue, as many as half the world's species of animals, plants and insects will become extinct. This is comparable to the last great extinction of the ice ages, in which

60% to 80% of the rest of the world's species disappeared.

And finally, I would add, our time is coming. Extinction does not happen only to other creatures. If we do not change our ways of living and thinking, it is slowly but without doubt coming to us.

The Power of Salt

On March 12, 1930, when the British still had a firm grip on India, Mahatma Gandhi and seventy-eight of his disciples strode out of Sabarmati ashram toward the sea. In the twenty-four days that followed, they walked two hundred miles, picking up more and more companions as village after village turned out to cheer the Mahatma and raise the new Indian flag. By the time they reached their destination, the seashore at Dandi, the group numbered several thousand.

Earlier in March, Gandhi had sent a letter to the British viceroy protesting the Salt Act, which forbade Indians to make their own salt and left them dependent on a British monopoly for what is, in a tropical country, a necessity of life. The viceroy did not reply. To Gandhi, this was the "opportunity of a lifetime." On the morning of April 6, before a huge crowd including reporters from around the world, Gandhi walked to the edge of the sea, picked up a pinch of salt, and set India free.

It was Gandhi's genius to recognize that although the British had the power to establish a monopoly on salt, they could maintain that monopoly only with the cooperation of the Indian people. With his inspiration and guidance, millions of ordinary individuals changed their lives in a small but powerful way: they stopped buying salt from the British and began making it themselves. Almost immediately, Indians along the coast and across the country were making, buying, and using homemade salt. A hundred thousand were jailed, and many more suffered great hardships, but throughout the campaign, millions of Indians refused steadfastly and without violence to depend on the British for salt. This brilliant campaign, which restored India's confidence in herself, was the turning point in her long struggle for independence. Afterward India knew she was free, and nothing the British did could halt her march toward freedom.

Today, in a modern industrial society like the United States, our most pressing need is not for salt or clothing or shelter. For most of us, as that advertising executive said, all our basic needs have been met. But there remains a hunger for something more. We want to *be* somebody. We want to feel secure. We want to love. Without any better way to satisfy these inner needs, we end up depending on possessions and profit – not just for our physical well-being but as a substitute for the dignity, fulfillment, and security we want so much. Because we still believe happiness lies in remaking the world around us, we look for inner fulfillment outside ourselves, and this makes us easy prey for manipulation.

My grandmother, if she were here to comment, might say, "If you have lost your freedom, what does it matter if you have a big car? What does it matter if you are a millionaire? You are not free." It seems to me that Americans, with their long history of freedom, should be especially sensitive to this loss. America's success at throwing off the shackles of colonialism was a great inspiration to us during our own struggle for independence.

Indeed, at the height of the salt campaign, when people were making salt and selling it on every street corner, Gandhi went to negotiate with Lord Irwin, viceroy of India. At teatime, Gandhi brought out a paper bag and, before the viceroy's astonished eyes, dropped some of its contents into his cup. "I will put a little of this salt into my tea," he explained mischievously, "to remind us of the famous Boston Tea Party." Despite all the trouble Gandhi was causing him, Lord Irwin could not resist joining in his laughter.

How, then, shall we free ourselves?

Let's start in little ways, by trying to make the connection between what we know to be healthy for our planet and what we do in our daily lives. As many environmentalists have suggested, we could walk instead of taking the car, or carpool or use mass transit instead of driving alone – that would be a small salt march in itself, with the added benefit that the commute would not be so lonely or expensive or long. We could start buying organic vegetables; if possible, we might even grow them in our own backyards, using no pesticides or other harmful chemicals. That would be the modern equivalent of making salt. We would be healthier, and so would the topsoil.

Today, even small changes like these seem very difficult. We all have so little time to spare; and we ask ourselves, what good would it do anyway? This is understandable. Without Gandhi's example, I think few Indians could have been persuaded that the British would be ushered out of India peacefully and gently and that a new independent nation of India would be founded – all by the power of salt.

How could one man have accomplished so much? From what hidden source did he draw his inspiration, his perseverance, his creativity? My visit to Mahatma Gandhi had only deepened my curiosity about this man who called himself an ordinary individual but who, by changing himself, had sparked such courage in a nation discouraged and frustrated for more than four hundred years. I could see now that it would take more time and work than I had expected to even begin to grasp his full significance. "My life is my message," Gandhi once wrote, and to all of us who wanted to share his work and ideals, that message was a resounding challenge: The only way to understand me, he was saying, is to go this way yourself.

The Hypothesis

> *The tree which moves some to tears of joy is in the eyes of others only a green thing that stands in the way.*
> — *William Blake*

Gandhi's life and achievements had exploded all my conceptions of what a human being could and could not do. The old limits no longer seemed to apply. As I cast about for a new understanding of who I was and where the world was going, I discovered two guides very near at hand. The first, of course, was the experience of growing up with my grandmother. I began to realize just how comprehensive her vision of the universe had been, and how patiently and lovingly she had introduced me to it.

The other was the guide Gandhi himself had followed. In the hundreds of letters he received each week, Gandhi was often asked how he had been able to change himself so completely, and his answer was always the same. He owed everything, he would say, to the Bhagavad Gita, his "spiritual reference book." The Bhagavad Gita is a short Sanskrit work of seven hundred verses that has fascinated and inspired mystics, physicists, psychologists, and philosophers of many countries for three thousand years. Set on a battlefield on the morning before a fierce battle, the Gita uses warfare as a metaphor for our personal battles with the challenges of life.

The Gita's message is simple but profound: our native state is freedom. What we want most from life is to be free of all the mental compulsions that keep us from living in peace with ourselves, with others, and with the environment. This desire for freedom is at the core of our personality, says the Gita, and our failings – whether they be insensitivity to the suffering of others, or greed, or anger, or fear, or any of the seven ailments Gandhi diagnosed – only hide our real nature like dust obscuring the face of a mirror.

I had read the Gita before, but it was not until I saw Gandhi that I understood its magnificent practicality. The Gita, I began to understand, was not just philosophy or poetry but a blueprint for the remaking of the human personality. I had been familiar with it since childhood, but I had never before read it in quite this way. Despite the fact that Gandhi seemed to tower above me like the Himalayas, I decided to put to the test his claim that anyone can undertake the same process of self-transformation.

I was not entirely sure he was right. Since my high school days, I had placed my faith in the cultural and intellectual achievements of the West – achievements that seemed to conflict with Gandhi's compassionate perspective. As a professor and writer, I had no desire to compromise my intellect; yet after years of searching, I did know one thing for certain: the emptiness of modern life was no longer enough, and would never be enough. What a paltry thing it seemed to live – however pleasantly, however successfully – and then to die without having found something of permanent value, without ever knowing why I had lived, without leaving the world a little better for my having lived.

I felt I had exhausted all the options life had to offer. Yet, as I reread the Gita, I realized there was one direction in which I had not searched. With the energy and desire I had formerly spent on the thousand and one things of life, I began to turn inward.

You could call it a gamble. Or, to put it in the language of science, you could say I adopted a new hypothesis. For the purpose of delving deeper into the meaning of my life, I placed my faith – all the faith I had formerly placed in literature and the achievements of the industrial era – in the Gita's hypothesis that what I was seeking rested not outside me but within, in the depths of my own heart and consciousness.

"Hypothesis is the most important mental technique of the investigator," writes the Cambridge professor W. I. B. Beveridge in his book *The Art of Scientific Investigation*, "and its main function is to suggest new experiments or new observations. Indeed, most experiments and many observations are carried out with the deliberate object of testing an hypothesis."

"Testing an hypothesis." That is exactly what I began to do, following in Gandhi's footsteps. Gandhi himself was a relentless experimenter who would not rest until he had found a beneficial purpose for every detail of his life. In fact, he subtitled his autobiography "The Story of My Experiments with Truth."

The Gita's hypothesis is that it is possible, by mastering the thinking process, to leave behind every unwanted habit and negative thought. To accomplish this, the Gita outlines a daily course of training in which we acquire conscious control of our attention, strengthening our will at such a deep level of the unconscious that no compulsive desire or addiction can sweep us away. What is the predicted result? When your will is linked to your intellect at the very depths of your personality, you discover yourself as you really are – secure, wise, compassionate, and intimately connected with all of life.

I was accustomed to thinking of myself as a learned man, relatively adept in a wide variety of mental activities, so this simple skill of gaining control over my attention seemed well within my grasp. It came as quite a surprise to see how little control I actually had. I discovered that my mind was like a titanic factory, engaged night and day in activities that were, for the most part, neither useful nor voluntary. When I tried to turn my attention away from the things I was used to thinking about – such as the topic of my next lecture or what had been said at the afternoon faculty meeting – and direct it inward, I was frustrated time and again.

Nevertheless, through diligent practice I began to bring a measure of control to my thinking process. More and more frequently there came times when, instead of being told by my conditioning what to think and how to act, I was the one who told my mind what to think. I found that I could maintain my peace of mind, even under trying circumstances.

To give you just one instance – one of my colleagues, who was probably a better scholar than I, didn't appreciate my passion for George Bernard Shaw. Whenever I was present in the faculty room, he would make some objectionable remark about Shaw, and I used to get upset, which seemed to please him. If I told him, "Must you say such things?" he would only respond, "I am not talking about you. I am talking about Bernard Shaw. Why should that bother you? You're not an Irishman – or are you?"

Once I had gained a little control over my thinking process, though, I learned how to detach myself from my opinions. One day, my colleague came in and sat in his chair, looking straight at me across the room. I could tell that he had a razor-sharp criticism prepared, but instead of shrinking into my collar, I got up, went over, and sat down by his side. "Well, what did you think of last night's production of Shaw's *Man and Superman*?" I asked him, and listened respectfully to everything he had to say. He couldn't quite believe it. I can't say we became good friends, but the atmosphere in the faculty room did get quite a bit clearer.

Before long I began to enlarge the scope of my experimentation: no part of my life was off limits to the testing and retesting of the Gita's hypothesis. I was surprised at how malleable my life became, as habits and patterns of behavior that had seemed permanent came under my conscious control.

Gradually, all my energy began to flow into this process. The results changed the way I lived – and the way I saw the universe. Beveridge goes on to say: "Another function [of an hypothesis] is to help one see the significance of an object or event that otherwise would mean nothing." My experiments were doing just that. My own life; the lives of others around me; the earth; the universe itself, which had seemed a mere "concatenation of atoms," now began to reveal a cohesiveness, compassionate wisdom, and purpose that until then I had seen only in my grandmother's life.

The Instrument of Observation

In comprehending the universe, according to the Gita, our primary instrument of observation is the mind. More than telescopes and microscopes – more even than our eyes and ears – our mind, gathering data through the senses and developing an interpretation of them, plays the central role in deciding what our universe looks like.

This is a rather abstract idea, so let me illustrate with a little story from my childhood. When I was growing up, the scouting movement had just come to India, and my friends and I all joined. We were much like Boy Scouts everywhere, I suppose – except that we wore green turbans in place of caps, and our expeditions took us to the tropical rain forest a few miles from our village.

For these expeditions, our scoutmaster would hire a certain local forester to be our guide. He was a great favorite with us. Although he had never learned to read or write, this man had spent his entire life in the forest and knew its every path and stream and watering hole. What fascinated us most about him was his intimate knowledge of the animals that lived there. He would talk for hours about deer and elephants as if they were members of his own family.

On one of these trips, when we had followed him about a mile into the forest, we stopped at the edge of a stream. He whispered to us, "Now listen carefully, with all your concentration. Don't be deceived by the rustling of leaves and the murmur of the brook. Something is coming this way. Can you hear?" We all strained our ears without result. After a few moments he told us, "A herd of deer is heading toward this very spot."

We laughed, but he went on to describe how many deer there were, how fast they were coming, and from which direction. Ten minutes later they appeared, cautiously making their way past us, exactly as he had described them.

Then he said, "Do you hear anyone drinking water?" We listened harder this time, but we still couldn't pick up a thing. "Just past those trees over there," he said, "about twenty wild elephants are drinking water and playing." Still not quite convinced, we followed him into a clearing. A few hundred yards away we saw a sight I shall never forget: in a large watering hole, several families of elephants were drinking water, washing, spraying, and playing like children. Fascinated, we all sat down and watched for a long time.

Finally, as the sun was beginning to set, our guide turned to us with a grin and said he had one more thing to show us – something that would top all his other feats. "Just listen to this. I can imitate the mating call of the tiger! One call, and all the tigers in the forest will be here in a minute." At that point we felt we had seen enough of his abilities. The scoutmaster, who was probably remembering that he would have to face our parents back in the village, said, "I think it's time for us to be starting back. The boys are getting hungry . . ."

Why couldn't we hear the deer or the elephants? We were all young and in good health, and there was nothing wrong with our ears. Surely those sounds had registered on our eardrums; yet we had heard nothing.

According to the Gita, the lack was not in the capacity of our ears but in our minds. People see and hear the things they pay attention to, and they pay attention to the things they know and love. Because our guide had lived all his life with those animals and loved them, his attention was naturally drawn to them. Amid the thousands of sounds that surrounded us – the birds calling, the wind blowing, the cicadas chirping, the monkeys chattering, the leaves and branches falling – he could hear the sound of a deer's delicate hoof picking its way through the underbrush, or the strange hollow sound of an elephant's trunk sucking up water.

As I continued to follow the Gita's suggestions and acquired a little more conscious control over my thinking, I began to suspect that most of the industrial era's problems arise because of where we are fixing our attention. For us, trying to see compassion in the world around us is as difficult as it was for me to hear the sound of the deer. Somehow, we have become so attuned to the sound and sight of profit that we can spot it anywhere, but we find it hard to recognize things like cooperation or compassion – even when they are awakening in our own hearts.

The trouble lies in our mental habits. The mind, our instrument of observation, is deeply influenced by the compulsive habits and addictions that characterize so much of modern life. Comparing the mind to a camera, you could say that these habits skew the focus, alter the depth of field, and in general do all they can to make us see not what is really there but what the mind wants us to see. And what it wants us to see is the profit or momentary gratification it is interested in, whether it is a pastry or a sports car, a promotion or a dividend. When our attention is glued to these things, we see only the fragmented, turbulent surface of life, not the vast, interconnected web of relationships supporting that surface.

A profit-seeking mind rarely misses an opportunity for profit or convenience, but it misses opportunities for cooperation and communication by the millions. To such a mind, a forest is not a home for deer and elephants – it is real estate. In the words of William Blake, "The tree which moves some to tears of joy is in the eyes of others only a green thing that stands in the way."

When we are absorbed in the pursuit of profit, we live in the narrow world of the bottom line. In that world, our only neighbors are buyers and sellers, our only concerns property, profit, and possessions. Yet all around us is a world teeming with people, animals, organisms, and elements – a deeply interconnected environment that responds to all we do to it. The world seems hostile and lifeless, and we seem insignificant in it, because, like the elephant, we look at it through such tiny eyes. Through those small eyes, shrunken by the desire for profit and personal gratification, we appear just as insignificant as all the green things – and all the other human beings, animals, fish, birds, and insects – that stand in the way.

Around the world, rain forests like the one near my village are host to roughly half the earth's plant, insect, and animal species. Through sixty-five million years of uninterrupted evolution, untouched by the climatic changes of the ice ages, rain forests have developed a complex system of interrelationships in which each species depends on the existence and activities of many others. In these relationships between animals and environment, animals and plants, animals and other animals, biologists have found abundant evidence of nature's thrift and compassion.

Everywhere, she exhibits the timing and delicate understanding of an artist, using endless creativity to provide a home and food for every creature, no matter how big or small. In the rain forest, as everywhere in nature, researchers have found that competition – "the law of the jungle" – is not nearly so important as the countless processes by which nature *avoids* competition. Here is the ecologist Paul Colinvaux:

> Whenever we find rather similar animals living together in the wild, we do not think of competition by tooth and claw, we ask ourselves, instead, how competition is avoided. When we find many animals apparently sharing a food supply, we do not talk of struggles for survival; we watch to see by what trick the animals manage to be peaceful in their coexistence.

And even among the trees and flowers, notes plant physiologist Frits Went, cooperation is the keynote:

> There is no violent struggle between plants, no warlike mutual killing, but a harmonious development on a share-and-share basis. The cooperative principle is stronger than the competitive one. . . . The forest giants among the trees do not kill the small fry under them. They hold back their development, and they prevent further germination. In a mountain forest in Java it was observed that the small trees living in the shade of the forest giants had not grown after 40 years, but they were still alive.

We have also learned a great deal about nature's innate thriftiness from the rain forest. Its richness and diversity are not due to the quality of its topsoil, which is usually quite poor, but to the extraordinary interaction of millions of different species, as they recycle water, nutrients, and minerals, and ensure that every resource is preserved and reused endlessly.

Finally, the forests have provided us with tantalizing glimpses of nature's compassion; one of my favorites is an observation by the researcher Jean-Pierre Hallet. Hallet was studying elephants in the Belgian Congo when he noticed an elephant that had lost its trunk, probably through some injury. Hallet was intrigued by the animal's svelte, well-fed appearance – without a trunk, an elephant has no tool for foraging. He followed the elephant and his herd into the forest. When the group finally settled down to browse for food, the mystery was solved: as the trunkless elephant stood by, the rest of the herd industriously tore off leaves and twigs for him. One at a time they brought bundles of food, playfully competing for the right to feed him. Not one of the elephants ate until their trunkless companion had eaten his fill.

Though we seldom realize it, we too are part of the rain forest. Even if we live thousands of miles from the nearest tropical zone, our lives are connected to the rain forest by many invisible links.

One of those links is the vital role that tropical plants play in modern medicine; a fourth of all our medicines are derived from them. Indeed, for thousands of years forests have been recognized as a great resource for healing. A significant story is told about one of the greatest figures in the history of medicine, the physician Jivaka, who is said to have served as the Buddha's personal physician. Before graduating from the ancient Indian equivalent of Harvard Medical School, Jivaka and his classmates were given a final examination. Each was handed a basket and sent into the forest to bring back any herbs or plants that had no medicinal use. All the other interns brought back armfuls of flowers and leaves, but Jivaka returned empty-handed. When he came before his surprised teacher, he explained: "We may not know it yet, but there is a use for every tree, herb, plant, and flower in the forest."

Twenty-five hundred years later, we still know little about the mysterious, promising world of the rain forest – but what we do know is astonishing. After testing less than one tenth of the species present, biologists have found that at least fourteen hundred tropical plant species contain substances active against cancer; and they suspect that rain forests may contain many plants with the potential to treat still-unconquered diseases, like AIDS.

Undoubtedly, many more generations of scientists could spend their lives exploring the rain forests and we would still know only a fraction. Edward O. Wilson, the noted Harvard biologist, estimates that it would require 25,000 researchers just to document the unknown species. Yet it is no longer certain that those generations – the scientists and doctors our children will grow up to be – will have that chance.

When I returned by train to my village many years after leaving for college, I passed through the area my fellow Scouts and I used to explore. I kept looking for the old, familiar landmarks – the spot where the forester lived; the stretch of forest where the elephants bathed and all those birds, insects, and flowers flourished. They were all gone. In their place stood miles and miles of factories, slums of all kinds, and the urban sprawl that has become synonymous with the word "progress."

This is a tragedy which has become commonplace in tropical countries around the globe. Each day, the world loses more than seventy-six thousand acres of tropical rain forest – that is over twenty-seven million acres each year. Much of the cleared land is used to raise cattle for beef or to support short-term agriculture, both of which quickly exhaust the already-poor soil. Ranchers and farmers then move on to cut and burn more acreage. With each acre, they burn not only trees but the myriad species of insects, birds, plants, and animals that have lived and evolved on that spot for sixty-five million years. As these species disappear into extinction, so do many of the indigenous peoples who have made their modest, harmonious homes in these tropical forests.

For a long time we have assumed that such problems were the responsibility of other governments and other people, but now ecologists tell us that wherever we live, they are *our* problems. Atmospheric scientists suspect that the loss of so much rain forest will dramatically disrupt the world's weather patterns. Already, in my native state of Kerala, some of the monsoon rains that made my state so prosperous are falling into the sea – probably because of weather changes caused by deforestation. And in our own hemisphere, a small but poignant indicator of our link with the rain forests has recently appeared as scientists have discovered that the population of songbirds on the East Coast of the United States has begun to decrease. One of the suspected reasons: these warblers, orioles, and other songbirds need the Central and South American rain forests as a winter home, and much of it has disappeared.

But worst of all, at least as far as human beings are concerned, is the fact that the burning of tropical rain forests is responsible for about twenty percent of the world's carbon dioxide emissions. Carbon dioxide is chief among the gases that create the "Greenhouse effect," the dangerous buildup of heat-trapping gases in the Earth's atmosphere . Due to the burning of fossil fuels and rain forest, the greenhouse effect may raise the temperature of the earth's atmosphere by between three and nine degrees Fahrenheit over the next sixty years.

That may not seem like much, but the effects on our environment – the environment our children will live in sixty years from now – could be devastating. It could turn our richest farmland into desert. By melting the polar ice caps, it could raise the world's sea level and flood whole cities. And such a rise in the earth's temperature could decimate or destroy our own forests, which could not survive such a rapid temperature change.

So we are part of the rain forest – but not just because its destruction affects us. The way we live also affects its survival: a great deal of the destruction in Central and South America is due to clear-cutting by wealthy landowners and multinational corporations eager to cash in on the developed world's appetite for beef; in Southeast Asia, there is money to be made exporting timber to Japan; in the Caribbean, forests are being decimated to create tourist centers. To a great extent, it is the appetites and addictions of industrial society which are destroying one of our greatest evolutionary resources.

Yet, in the Gita's compassionate perspective, the problem is not us, but the conditioning which has limited our instrument of observation. When we are in the grip of an addiction – to profit, to convenience, to our cars – we see only what contributes to resolving our immediate problem: how to make more money, how to produce more energy, how to save a little time. This conditioning restricts our vision to the object of our desire, be it a hamburger or a trip to the mall or a quarterly profit, while the long-range consequences are ignored, left for another day, another nation, another generation to cope with. We may dimly perceive the broader implications, but under the pressure of time and competition, we don't have a chance to think them out.

Beyond this thick fog of conditioning lies a universe ruled not by competition and division but by symbiosis and cooperation, a universe built on interrelationships. The science of ecology teaches us that everything in the universe is connected. We cannot separate ourselves from the consequences of even the least of our actions: whatever we do *here* comes back *there*. This is the law of the unity of life. Like gravity or any other law of nature, you cannot break it; you can only break yourself against it. If you throw a bottle in the air, it will return to earth and break. Similarly, if you act in a way that violates the unity of life – polluting the atmosphere, wasting precious resources, ignoring the needs of others – you will find your health, your peace of mind, and your happiness destroyed. We are not separate fragments. Like the songbird, and all the other animals and plants that are part of the rain forest, we depend on each other and on the environment.

"In ecology, as in economics," wrote Barry Commoner in the early seventies,

> . . . every gain is won at some cost. . . . Because the global ecosystem is a connected whole, in which nothing can be gained or lost and which is not subject to over-all improvement, anything extracted from it by human effort must be replaced. Payment of this price cannot be avoided; it can only be delayed. The present environmental crisis is a warning that we have delayed nearly too long.

A statement like this reminds me of those signs you see on the freeway: "Go back. You're going the wrong way." Biologists and ecologists like Dr. Commoner have played an important part in examining the dangers of our present way of life and posting such warning signs. Our industrial way of life, they tell us, has made our Mother Earth sick; the global warming is a terrible fever that will ravage her health if we do not change our ways of driving, buying, eating, and living.

During the next few decades, I believe, scientists will be instrumental in showing us the connections between our daily lives and the environment, in helping us find non-invasive, nonpolluting alternative energy sources, and in exploring and defending the world's great resources, such as the tropical forests. We need good science more than ever. As John Eddy of the University Corporation for Atmospheric Research puts it "We've got to get the planet into intensive care, [and] start to monitor its vital signs."

Many young scientists are eager to work on such projects, yet they find it difficult to obtain the financial and institutional support they need to carry on their work. Instead, a great deal of this precious support goes to projects that at best do nothing to serve humanity or the rest of life, and at worst have the potential to destroy our world even before the greenhouse effect can touch us. Around the world, roughly a quarter of all research and development funds goes to the science of war.

Science Without Humanity

Where are we going with our science and our business, our politics and our economic theories? What do we really want to accomplish, and why? How will our innovations affect life as a whole? These questions should be posted not only on the doors to our boardrooms and laboratories but on the doors to our minds and hearts.

Wernher von Braun said, "If you know the laws of space and obey them, space will treat you kindly." So it is with the law of the unity of life. We have invested much time and energy exploring the physical laws of nature and inventing ingenious applications of them, but we have taken little time to consider in what direction those applications will take us. This long-term perspective is the vital foundation our science and business lack today. Without an ever-alert conscience steering us toward constructive, positive research and sounding an alarm each time we waver in our respect for life as a whole, we are in grave danger of being swept off our feet by forces we only dimly perceive.

The Manhattan Project is a sobering example of the very best of science serving the motivations that drive men to war, with unimaginably destructive consequences. Errors like this do not occur because science is destructive or scientists are evil, but because we have limited our investigations to just half the things we need for health and peace: we study how to remake the world, but not how to remake ourselves. The result is what Gandhi calls science without humanity.

Let me make it clear that the science I am referring to is not just what is done in laboratories by people in white coats. It is the responsibility of each one of us. In the first place, it is we, with our votes and our purchases, who decide which projects are funded and which are not, which corporations are successful and which are not. If we wanted to, we could tell the Pentagon, as some young people have suggested, "We think you presently have quite enough destructive technology. If you want more, have a bake sale."

But second, and even more important, we are all technicians. Technology shapes our lives in a thousand subtle ways, and we in turn affect our world with the machines technology gives us. Today the average person in the developed world owns dozens of machines that consume energy, emit gases, discharge effluents, and release chemical wastes the likes of which nature has never seen. You might think of the average household as a microlaboratory; together with millions of other scientists in similar microlaboratories, we are conducting a large-scale experiment on ourselves and our world. The hypothesis? By the constant and universal application of technology, we can improve the quality of our lives; by producing and consuming more and more things, we can find inner fulfillment.

It is a tribute to the energy and drive of modern society that so many people are working around the clock to test this hypothesis. Unfortunately, as the data come in, there are indications that the hypothesis is faulty. We have never had more cars and machines to "save time," but we have also never had to spend two to three hours a day commuting in a car filled with toxic fumes. We have never before had such excellent medical equipment, but neither have we had such pollution to endanger our health. We have never before had nuclear power. We have never before had nuclear accidents.

What do we really want to accomplish with our technology and business, and why? How will our innovations affect life as a whole? If we were careful to ask these questions every time we embarked on a project, we would find that we always have a choice between two kinds of science. I read recently of a vivid example of these two sciences, personified in two scientists: each talented and capable, but each leaving us a vastly different legacy.

The first is Thomas Midgley, who in 1930 was asked by the Frigidaire division of General Motors to find something to replace the toxic ammonia being used in refrigerators. Midgley came up with one of commercial science's biggest success stories: chlorofluorocarbons, now commonly known as CFCs.

Midgley's chemical compound was welcomed as a miracle. Soon similar substances were being used widely in industry as aerosol propellants and refrigerants. I understand that today, three fourths of the food consumed in this country is cooled by chlorofluorocarbons. We depend on them for air-conditioning, as solvents in the electronics industry, as an ingredient in fumigants and pesticides, and in the ubiquitous plastic foams we use for insulation, cushions, egg cartons, fast food containers, and padded dashboards in cars.

By 1973, in the United States alone, eight hundred and fifty million pounds of CFCs were being produced annually. That was the year when a second scientist, Sherwood Rowland, began investigating how CFCs behave in the atmosphere. Until then, little was known about the effects of CFCs. By June of 1974, Rowland, along with Mario Molina of Berkeley, had published a paper in *Nature* magazine. They had made a momentous discovery, but, as Rowland says, "There was no moment when I yelled 'Eureka!' I just came home one night and told my wife, 'The work is going very well, but it looks like the end of the world.'"

By now, what they had discovered is common knowledge. CFCs are extremely hardy substances – some compounds remain in the lower atmosphere for seventy-five to one hundred and twenty years. Slowly, as more and more are released, they drift upward ten to twenty miles above the earth, where they break down under ultraviolet radiation and release chlorine atoms, each of which can destroy up to a hundred thousand ozone molecules before it eventually falls back to earth. The most dramatic demonstration of the damage CFCs have done is the huge hole in the ozone layer – roughly the size of the continental United States – that has begun to appear each fall above the Antarctic.

This phenomenon may seem rather distant, but its effects are not. Because our ecosystem depends so much on cooperation and interdependence, a change like this, even high above the earth, has the capacity to wreak havoc with all of life – to become, in Tennyson's phrase, "the little rift within the lute that by and by will make the music mute, and ever widening slowly silence all."

The ozone layer, produced by the interaction of sunlight and oxygen molecules, shields us from a great deal of the sun's ultraviolet radiation – radiation that, if not blocked, can do terrible damage to life on earth. Skin cancer is the most immediate and obvious hazard to human beings, but excessive ultraviolet radiation can also lead to cataracts and, as some researchers have speculated, may cause severe damage to the body's immune system.

But these are only the immediate threats, and humans are not the only living creatures to be affected. All forms of life depend on the delicate balance of light and radiation provided by the ozone layer. Over thousands of centuries, the earth's ecosystem has evolved a network of interactions and adaptive mechanisms perfectly suited to this balance. A sudden change, such as a dramatic rise in ultraviolet radiation, might endanger the entire system. If we do not act quickly to curb the use of CFCs, it is hard to predict or even imagine the effect on our agriculture, or on the marine food chain, or on the billions of acres of forest that stabilize our climate.

So we see two scientists, Midgley and Rowland, both excellent at what they do and both sincerely following their profession. I do not doubt that the late Mr. Midgley believed he was making a positive contribution to the world. Yet the success of Midgley's research has helped make the earth a much more dangerous place, while Rowland's success has alerted us to that danger and given us a chance to save the earth for our children.

Although we are rarely aware of it, we have a choice: will we invent new chemicals designed solely to produce a profit – under the pressure of competition with other countries, manufacturers, or scientists, and barely considering their possible side effects – or will we do research that respects the organic processes of nature and contributes to life as a whole? Will we apply our genius to developing X-ray laser missile "defenses" or to defending the immune systems of the world's children? Until we train our minds to be relatively free from addiction to profit, power, and individual self-gratification, we will always waver as we do today: one moment contributing things and ideas of value, the next doing irreparable harm to ourselves and others.

Let me repeat: I am not speaking only to those who pursue science as a profession. We all bear responsibility for the accomplishments of science, since we all support it – financially, with our purchases and taxes, and in our mental habits, where we depend on technology for profit, prestige, and convenience. We are the ones who are responsible for deforestation, global warming, and depletion of the ozone layer, but if we do not make the necessary changes, it will be our children and grandchildren who face the consequences.

The atmospheric scientist Michael Oppenheimer puts it with the frankness I have come to appreciate in Americans:

We're flying blind into a highly uncertain future. These changes are going to affect every human being and every ecosystem on the face of the earth, and we only have a glimmer of what these changes will be. The atmosphere is supposed to do two things for us: maintain a constant chemical climate of oxygen, nitrogen and water vapor, and help maintain the radiation balance – for example, by keeping out excess ultraviolet. The unthinkable is that we're distorting this atmospheric balance. We're shifting the chemical balance so that we have more poisons in the atmosphere – ozone and acid rain on ground level – while we're also changing the thermal climate of the earth through the greenhouse effect and – get this – simultaneously causing destruction of our primary filter of ultraviolet light. It's incredible. Talk about the national-debt crisis – we're piling up debts in the atmosphere, and the piper will want to be paid.

An Alternative Hypothesis

When we begin to study a phenomenon, we do not actually know what we are studying. In order to learn more about it, we formulate an hypothesis. It is important to keep in mind, however, that until we thoroughly test our hypothesis, and compare the results of our experiments with its predictions, we are not on solid ground. Of course, where there are gaps in our knowledge we must have an hypothesis, but we must also test that hypothesis – rigorously and with an uncompromising regard for the truth. Where the hypothesis is inaccurate, we must do more research.

The hypothesis of industrial civilization was that by acquiring and consuming more things we would become happy, fulfilled, and healthy. Every day this seems less likely. As I look back, I wonder how I could ever have been taken in by the belief that each of us is a separate speck in a universe of insignificant, competing fragments. There is so little to recommend this view; yet I, like almost everyone else influenced by industrial conditioning, had unquestioningly based my life on it. Now it is clear to me that this assumption, which has been presented with authority as the truth, the fruit of centuries of scientific investigation, is only a hypothesis.

We have an alternative: a different hypothesis of who we are and how we fit into the universe. This different image of the human being and the world, which I shall present in the second and third sections of this book, does not contradict the findings of science. It simply asks that we carry our investigations further, into the deeper sources of our actions. Up to now, we have learned well how to serve our addiction to profit, but we have not learned how to serve our long-range health and well-being. We have not learned who we are or why we are here. We have unnecessarily limited our science – and ourselves.

The hypothesis of a compassionate universe is not new, nor is the investigation I am proposing. It has been suggested before, at many times, in many places, and by many great and eloquent voices. What is different now is our unprecedented opportunity to test it in every aspect of life. Indeed, as the only creatures on earth who have the power – and, it sometimes seems, the inclination – to bring life on this planet to an end, it is our responsibility to test the hypothesis as it has never been tested before. The choice is ours. It can only be made by each of us, one at a time, one day at a time, but the results will shape the lives of our children and our children's children for centuries to come. Our choice, I hope, will ensure that those centuries will come in peace and harmony and those children will flourish.

Part Two / A Higher Image

The alternative hypothesis was enunciated twenty-five hundred years ago in the Bhagavad Gita, and can be found at the core of every one of the world's great religious traditions: beneath the surface level of conditioned thinking in every one of us there is a single living spirit. The still small voice whispering to me in the depths of my consciousness is saying exactly the same thing as the voice whispering to you in your consciousness. "I want an earth that is healthy, a world at peace, and a heart filled with love." It doesn't matter if your skin is brown or white or black, or whether you speak English, Japanese, or Malayalam – the voice, says the Gita, is the same in every creature, and it comes from your true self.

Peeling Back
the Iron Mask

*He lives in wisdom who sees himself
in all and all in him.*
    – *Bhagavad Gita*

As the years have passed, I have often reflected on my visit to Mahatma Gandhi's ashram. In particular, there is one memory to which I have returned again and again.

I was sitting with the other visitors, resting after a long, brisk walk with Gandhiji. The sun had just dropped below the horizon, and the broad central Indian sky was slowly taking on one bright hue after another. As the evening's first cool breeze drifted across the plain, Mahadev Desai, Gandhi's personal secretary, recited the last eighteen verses of the second chapter of the Bhagavad Gita. At the very first line, a change came over Gandhiji.

"He lives in wisdom who sees himself in all and all in him." Listening to these words, Gandhi became very still. "Not agitated by grief or hankering after pleasure, he lives free from lust and fear and anger." Watching him, I could almost feel the tremendous concentration he was focusing on the words. By the end of a few more lines, he had closed his eyes and was utterly absorbed. "He is forever free," recited his secretary, "who has broken out of the ego cage of *I* and *mine.*"

I had heard the Gita's description of a fully realized human being many times before; I had read it in Sanskrit and in English; I had heard it explained by scholars, philosophers, and pundits; but now, for the first time, I was not just hearing or reading those words – I was seeing them. Sitting beneath a small tree in front of us, legs folded, hands resting gently in his lap, was a man who really did see himself in all and all in him. From Gandhi's every gesture and word, from everything he was doing for India and the world, and above all from the deep inner peace we felt in his presence, it was clear that there was no dividing line between his happiness and ours. He had left behind every thought of "I" and "mine."

I had not found such a person in all the literature I had read, all the conferences and speeches I had attended. Yet this, I began to suspect, was exactly what I had been looking for. I had not lacked for comfort or prestige, but there was something more in me – something I had not yet understood – that was struggling to find expression in my life. For me, as for so many other young men and women in India and around the world, Gandhi had awakened the desire to grow. In the depths of my heart, I heard a quiet voice speaking to me: "This is what you really are. Do not settle for less . . . "

I have come to believe, from my own experience and my observations of others – particularly the young people of the United States – that when human beings reach a state in which their physical wants are more than satisfied, when the optimum level of material abundance and physical comfort is reached, something in us feels a sense of satiation akin to nausea. Absorbed up to then in the pursuit of prosperity and material security, we begin to feel restless, dissatisfied with the limits of life as it is being lived, constrained by the lack of challenges – and of love.

Then it becomes possible to hear a still, small voice speaking from deep below the conscious level of our mind, from beneath the level of conditioned desires. The voice was always there, but we were so busy with other things that we did not hear it. "I want an earth that is healthy, a world at peace, and a heart filled with love," it is saying. "I want my life to count."

When people begin to hear this voice, they need to seek out a goal worthy of their ambition. Otherwise, as I came to realize, the joy begins to ebb out of life. Confined to the realm of tiny, self-centered pleasures and irritations, the magnificent capacities of the human being – the energy and drive that can accomplish so much good – go to waste or turn self-destructive.

Modern life, especially as represented in the media, provides few such goals, and even fewer examples of people who strive for them. In an Indian movie I saw recently, a villager leaves home for the first time to travel to the city of Bombay. When he returns, his family and friends crowd around him, asking what it was like in the big city. His laconic reply sums up our era: "Such tall buildings . . . and such small people."

If we were asked to give an accounting of our society's achievements, we could claim many great technological developments and scientific discoveries, plenty of sky-scrapers, and the amassment of huge sums of money, but few truly secure, truly wise, truly great men and women. It is not for lack of ability or energy, though; there is simply nothing to strive for. To grow to our full height, we need to be challenged with tasks that draw out our deeper re-sources, the talents and capacities we did not know we had. We need to be faced with obstacles that cannot be sur-mounted unless we summon up every last ounce of our daring and creativity. This kind of challenge is familiar to any great athlete or scientist or artist. Those I have spoken with all agree that no truly worthwhile accomplishment comes easily.

It is exactly this challenge that most young people hun-ger for today. Look at the Olympic Games, for example. Divers, skiers, runners, swimmers, gymnasts: these athletes work many hours a day, day in and day out, for years, making sacrifices and denying themselves things other teenagers crave – all for the sake of a distant and nearly impossible goal. But when the Olympics are over, and the medals are put away, and these daring young people pass into adulthood, what challenge does our society provide to draw out their courage and constructive energy? What do we have to offer these men and women who have glimpsed the joy of self-discipline and sacrifice?

The answer is, as I discovered for myself, very little. In almost every area of modern life, we direct our young people toward an ideal that is, to be charitable, utterly ridiculous.

Wealth Without Work

I remember the first time I went to a swimming pool here in the United States. I grew up a great lover of swimming. The river that separated our village from the next served as our swimming pool, and my friends and I would eagerly await the monsoon season – it was great sport for us to swim all the way to the other side, trying not to be pushed off course by the powerful flood current. You can understand my surprise, then, when I came to the pool and saw a young chap floating on an inner tube, sipping a soft drink. I had expected rows of energetic Americans swimming lap after lap, but all I found was this fellow drifting in the sun. As I spoke with him, it became clear that this was his idea of putting a swimming pool to its best use. He was really under the impression that he was having a grand time.

If we took a poll about Gandhi's seven social sins, I think few people would say they are in favor of science without humanity, or politics without principles. But it would not be hard to find quite a number who enthusiastically approve of wealth without work. Here is what a prominent Wall Street figure recently had to say in a commencement address at a major university: "Greed is all right. Greed is healthy. You can be greedy and still feel good about yourself." To judge by the images in the media and the assumptions implicit in our economic system, the ideal life for a member of our species is to lie on an air mattress sipping something long and cool — or to pursue any of the millions of equivalent pastimes Madison Avenue assures us are life's peak experiences.

Now, there is nothing wrong with floating in a pool, but there is also nothing in it that draws out the tremendous inner resources we inherit at our birth as human beings. So many of our finest young people, hungry for meaning and challenge, have explored every pleasure and ambition our society offers and found nothing worth their time and energy. Parents I have spoken with express bewilderment: now, when they are able to give their children a life that is no longer a precarious struggle for material security, a life that includes a higher education and many of life's luxuries, these children are turning to drugs or despairing of life altogether. In this country, one of the wealthiest on earth, it's estimated that five hundred thousand young people attempt suicide each year. To me, this is a sign that we have failed to find anything higher to strive for than a life of leisure.

Wealth without work can hardly even be called a goal. To condition young people to believe that a life of leisure is the height of fulfillment is to confine them to the lowest possible image of themselves, an image that leaves little room for growth or change. In effect, it is telling them they are incapable of anything but submitting blindly to the force of conditioning.

I am reminded of that Dumas story in which a heavy iron mask is locked around a young prince's head by his rivals. Wealth without work is a mask like that. For eyes, it has the thinnest of slits — only large enough to see profit and loss, excitement and boredom, personal satisfaction and frustration.

I grew up with a different understanding of wealth. Our village, as I have said, was prosperous. We lacked nothing, yet we had little of what most economists today call wealth.

A rich topsoil, nourished by centuries of village agriculture; one hundred inches of rain a year; a dense forest and plentiful coconut groves; a fresh, pure supply of water, which we drank straight from our wells – these were free, and they formed the material resources for our prosperity.

The real foundation for our prosperity, though, was the deep and enduring sense of community that enabled us to make the best use of those resources. On this foundation, a tradition of excellent craftsmanship had grown up. Generation after generation of potters, carpenters, blacksmiths, goldsmiths, and weavers learned their trades from their families. They took great pride in the beauty, utility, and enduring quality of their work.

So we had all the things we needed – well-crafted, beautiful things that lasted a long time – but we did not do much "consuming." The economist in the iron mask would not be impressed by our statistics. A quick look at our GNP and he would probably say, "A very backward state, more to be pitied than envied." In terms of gross national product, we were a nonentity.

The kind of economics that has predominated in the industrial era – what might be called "iron mask" economics – measures our standard of living not by how fulfilled and secure we are, nor by how well or how long our products last, nor by the health of our environment. These things are not even considered in the equation. According to the economist in the iron mask, prosperity is measured by how much we produce and consume. The implicit assumption should be familiar by now. It is the industrial hypothesis: the more we produce and consume, the more fulfilled and secure we will be.

By this hypothesis, we should be close to heaven – never before have so many people consumed so much. It has been taken to such an extreme that things are made and sold that have absolutely no purpose beyond making a profit or filling an empty hour. Shopping has become a pastime: people go to stores not to buy things but to look for things to buy. Millions of people spend all their capacity for devotion, imagination, and love on shopping. Those bumper stickers you see in the mall parking lots are only partly in jest: "Shop till you drop"; "I shop, therefore I am."

To me, it is a tragic scene. What these people are looking for – security, satisfying relationships, fulfillment – cannot be found in a new dress or car or diamond ring. These are only things; and things, it seems to me, are meant to be used, not loved. People are to be loved; animals are to be loved; the green earth is to be loved. According to our conditioning, it is just the reverse. Constantly, and in a thousand subtle ways, television, movies, and advertisers tell us the purpose of life is to love things and use people.

Under this pressure, we have allowed consumption to become the goal of our economy – and our lives. When we are depressed, we buy something to cheer ourselves up. When we are elated, we buy something to celebrate. When we are bored, we buy something just to buy something. If we were to look at all this in the bright light of common sense, we would see that, as the economist E. F. Schumacher puts it, consumption is not an end in itself; it is merely the means to an end. Its purpose is to ensure that we have what we need.

Schumacher gives us a logical guideline: "The aim should be to obtain the maximum of well-being with the minimum of consumption." This is solid common sense. "The cultivation and expansion of needs," he writes, "is the antithesis of wisdom. It is also the antithesis of freedom and peace. . . ." In a world of limited resources, we should use only what we need for a comfortable, secure, fulfilled life.

With that pungent but gentle wit that was one of his

trademarks, Gandhi once said that the multiplication of hospitals is not an indication of increased health. I would add, the multiplication of shopping centers is not an indication of increased prosperity – no matter what it does for our GNP. Nor is the multiplication of desires. Consumption is only one side of the coin. The other is that particular specialty of industrial civilization – the product that sets our age apart from all others – waste.

As any ecologist can tell you, waste is utterly unknown in nature. In everything she does, nature is thrifty and efficient – what one creature eats or uses is saved and used again by another. A consumption-oriented society, however, is a different matter. Our purpose is often nothing more than to extract as much profit in as little time as possible, with no interest in what we put back or save for the future. As a result, much of our industrial activity produces some form of waste that is either out of balance with the rest of nature or downright harmful, that benefits no one and cannot be used again. In terms of the global ecological balance it is a net loss, and a huge one. "One of the chief reasons for the present environmental crisis," wrote Dr. Commoner in the early seventies, "is that great amounts of materials have been extracted from the earth, converted into new forms, and discharged into the environment without taking into account [the ecological law] that 'everything has to go somewhere.' The result, too often, is the accumulation of harmful amounts of material in places where, in nature, they do not belong."

It might be more accurate to call our GNP the "garbage national product." We mine uranium, convert it to radioactive plutonium, and end up with vast quantities of nuclear waste that will take centuries to decay to a safe state. We plunder the earth's fossil fuel reserves, squander them in our factories and cars, and end up with air so filled with sulfur dioxide that our rain is toxic, killing the lakes and forests it used to nourish.

And then, of course, there are the petrochemical products we have incorporated into practically every aspect of our lives, from the food production process to the many household chemicals we use every week. Pouring into channels, rivers, and drainage ditches, spilling accidentally from factories and storage tanks, seeping through the water table, leaking from offshore oil rigs, being flushed directly onto the shoreline – in the end, tons and tons of motor oils, chemical fertilizers, herbicides, and pesticides find their way to the sea, upsetting one of the most delicate, and essential, of the ecosystems on which our life depends.

During the past thirty years, Jacques Cousteau has noted a dramatic decrease in marine life. "A dead sea means a dead earth," he warns, and recently those words have begun to sound even more ominous. In the spring and summer of 1988, an estimated three quarters of the seal population in the North Sea, the Irish Sea, and the Baltic Sea died in what some people are calling the Black Death of the sea. Many scientists suspect that the epidemic was caused by a severe weakening of the seals' immune systems from exposure to industrial pollution.

Indirectly, we all contribute to this destruction of the sea by our support of agribusiness products, by our purchases, and by our conditioned desire to consume. But each of us also contributes directly by the chemicals we pour down the sink and spray on our gardens and the garbage we throw away. I could hardly believe my eyes when I read recently that in California, where I live, each man, woman, and child discards an average of twenty-five pounds of garbage each week. This means that each person throws away well over half a ton of garbage every year. The result is a garbage crisis of extraordinary proportions. Our landfills are being exhausted, and as they deteriorate, they release many harmful chemicals, such as mercury from discarded batteries or cadmium from plastic containers, and these too find their way to the sea.

What we want most from wealth, I think, is security; yet the way we have gone about accumulating wealth has brought us just the opposite. In poisoning the sea, we are well on the way to poisoning ourselves.

It is time to put the industrial era, and its primitive, simplistic definition of human fulfillment, behind us. A country's real wealth is the ambitions and high ideals of its young people. When we add up the cost of any technological innovation or social activity, let us include the cost of damaged ideals. In terms of gross national product, a bomber or a missile project may be a plus, but for the young people who are hired to build it instead of protecting the rain forest or investigating solar power, it is a terrible minus. Advertising that conditions young people to love money and possessions more than people may send the GNP into the black, but it sends our real wealth far into the red.

The real wealth of a country is measured not by its gross national product but by its grand national philosophy, by the number of secure, wise, and generous people it has and by the health of its environment. These are what truly determine the quality of life. And these are the very things our present way of life is threatening to destroy.

Peeling Back the Mask

As I continued to test the Gita's hypothesis, I began to find little cracks in the iron mask – small places where, with great effort, I could peel back a little of the conditioning that convinces us we are separate from the rest of life. Through what I can only ascribe to my grandmother's wise and loving guidance, I was dazzled to catch a few glimpses of the radiant personality behind the mask. It was much more than I had ever thought possible, or hoped to become. I sensed that this was my own self, yet I shared it with all of life. In that figure I saw the best of every person and creature: I saw, for just a brief, tantalizing moment, that this is who we all really are. What I had been seeking was inside me – and inside everyone else – all along.

My grandmother, who lived in continuous awareness of this shining personality within and made her whole life a reflection of its light, had prepared me for this experience throughout my childhood and youth. With great artistry, she had taught me that life's only lasting joy comes in erasing the boundary line between "mine" and "yours."

Our capacity to give, to think of others' needs before our own, to love: as my grandmother saw it, these inner resources are our greatest wealth. Those who derive their security from external things like money or possessions or power are the only really poor people in this world. "Don't be a beggar from life," she often said to me. "Life has only contempt for beggars. If you tell life, 'I don't care what you bring me, so long as I have the opportunity to give,' life will take off its hat and say, 'How may I serve you, sir?'"

Granny rarely taught with words, though. More often she helped me discover these things for myself, as she did during the summer of my freshman year in college. My ambition at the time was to become a writer. Everybody said that if you want to write, you have to have experience, so I got the idea of wandering off to explore our corner of South India on foot and observing life firsthand. I got Granny's permission – actually, the idea was hers, but she made me think it was mine – and set out.

My paths led me to a rather small, hard-working village. Exploring on foot was the kind of thing an Englishman or

American might do, but for a fresh-faced Indian boy it was unusual: when I showed up suddenly in this isolated village, people must have thought I had dropped from Mars. Naturally they asked all sorts of questions, and when they found out I was a writer they were really impressed. No one among them had ever had a chance to learn to read or write.

Then someone got a bright idea: wouldn't I like to teach them?

I felt lost. I was younger than most of them; I had no teacher's training and not the faintest notion of how to begin. I had come out to observe life, and I was already in over my head.

"We have no money to pay you with," the villagers explained cheerfully. "But we can give you food and a roof over your head."

"Do you have a building we can use as a schoolroom?" I asked doubtfully.

"No," they replied, "but that's no problem. You just be ready to start tomorrow, and we'll make you a school."

"If you can do that," I said, "you can be sure I'll do my best to teach you." And that was the end of my walking tour.

There was a full moon that night. When I turned up at the proposed site, I found there was a boy or man there from every home in the village. We worked throughout the night. First we put up the mud walls, then the thatched roof. Next we covered the floor with sand, put up a little blackboard, and got a piece of rail from the station master to use as a bell. By early morning, the school was ready.

Most of the adults worked in the fields, so the children came to school in the daytime and the adults attended in the evening, after dinner. None of us had a watch or clock; to keep time, we listened for the train. Two trains passed by the village – one early in the evening and the other several hours later. When the first one came through, it was supposed to be time to stop. But I would become so absorbed in teaching that I wouldn't even hear the train, and my students wouldn't tell me, either. They all kept quiet. Then I would hear the second train and say, "There goes the Blue Mountain Express – it must be late!" "Oh, no, that's the Malabar Express," they would assure me.

They would bring me fruits and vegetables, sandals they made with their own hands, pieces of cloth that they wove right in their homes. I spent all my time with them; we worked hard in school, shared all our meals, and went swimming and climbing together on our days off.

By the end of the summer, they had learned the basics of reading, writing, and reckoning, which must have felt like the greatest achievement of their lives. Yet I felt I had learned much more. From those simple villagers, who had just the bare minimum of material possessions, I had learned that the reward of work is not financial but the joy of the work itself and the satisfaction of being deeply connected with the lives of those around you.

It seems to me that the young people of the developed world (I would call it the *over*developed world) are looking for just the kind of work I found that glorious summer in Tamil Nadu – work that tests the muscles of the will and deepens the capacity to love. This is the kind of work a human being is made for.

Wealth without work is more of a curse than most of us realize. When we are deprived of real work, we lose one of our greatest opportunities for inner growth. "If the nature of the work is properly appreciated and applied," wrote the modern Indian economist Kumarappa,

> it will stand in the same relation to the higher faculties as food is to the physical body. It nourishes and enlivens the

higher man and urges him to produce the best he is capable of. It directs his free will along the proper course and disciplines the animal in him into progressive channels. It furnishes an excellent background for man to display his scale of values and develop his personality."

Even for our physical well-being, according to the noted biologist Dr. Hans Selye, work is a necessity.

"It may be a necessity," says the man in the iron mask, "but it is an evil necessity. As far as I'm concerned, the less work the better." The man in the iron mask works only to pay his bills – or to become famous or rich or powerful. He works to beat the competition. The man in the iron mask is often stressed out; he needs vacations to recover from work.

My grandmother would not have called such activity work. Real work, in her eyes, is never a disagreeable chore. It contributes to life rather than taking from it; it gives us the chance to discover and hone our skills, to see how we fit into life, and to lose our sense of isolation by sharing a common goal with our fellow human beings.

I am not saying that this kind of work is easy; selfless work is the hardest work in the world. But every step of the way brings more power to help and serve those around us. Even a taste of such work brings a glimpse of what it means to live in a compassionate universe.

In fact, insofar as you can forget yourself and think of the needs of others, you *become* an expression of the compassionate universe. What you want, more and more, is to enrich the lives of everyone around you. When you work like this, you are never bored or out of a job – the world is filled with people who need your help. You are never lonely. How could you be? Your whole purpose is to draw closer to others, and that motivation cannot help but draw others to you. Who can resist such a person?

One of my favorite Indian stories is about a great king, Vipashcit, who worked this way his whole life. He devoted his reign to improving the welfare of his people, and they came to love and revere him more as a saint than as a king. When he died, it is said, an angel came to escort him to heaven. But King Vipashcit had an unusual request. "Before I enter eternal bliss," he asked, "may I see the suffering of those in hell?"

The angel was a bit surprised, but he agreed and led King Vipashcit into another realm. What the king saw there puzzled him. Wherever he walked, he saw only happy faces. People ran to greet him and receive his blessing; there were tears in their eyes, but they were tears of joy. A little taken aback, Viapshcit turned to his guide and asked, "Why have you brought me here directly? I wanted to visit the other place first."

"Your majesty," the angel replied respectfully, "this *is* the other place."

"I don't understand. I expected hell to be full of suffering."

"This world *is* full of suffering: behind you, beyond you, wherever you cannot see. It is being near you that fills these people with joy."

"Then," said Vipashcit, "I need go no further. I have found my heaven."

The Lesson of the Hummingbird

You see things; and you say, "Why?"
But I dream things that never were;
and I say "Why not?"
    – *George Bernard Shaw*

Often, as I eat my breakfast, I see a flash of iridescent orange zip by the kitchen window and hover in midair at the lip of a flower. A hummingbird threads its long, delicate bill into the center of the flower, not even touching the petals, and sips its breakfast. A moment later it is gone, having drunk only what was necessary and leaving the flower pollinated. Precise, efficient, agile, respectful: I think humanity can find no better teacher in the art of living.

To me, the hummingbird holds out a promise: this is how we all can live, gradually outgrowing a way of life in which we gulp down all the nectar, spoil the flower by pulling off the petals, and finally uproot the plant. "Such a way of life," writes E. F. Schumacher, referring to our overuse of fossil fuels, "could have no permanence and could therefore be justified only as a purely temporary expedient. As the world's resources of non-renewable fuels – coal, oil, and natural gas – are exceedingly unevenly distributed over the globe, and undoubtedly limited in quantity, it is clear that their exploitation at an ever-increasing rate is an act of violence against nature, which must almost inevitably lead to violence between men." The same could be said about any of our precious resources, from bauxite to rain forests.

To put it in economic terms, we are frittering away our capital when we should be living wisely on the interest, leaving the capital to bear rich dividends for future generations. This is what Gandhi meant by commerce without morality, a way of life in which all our nobler goals and aspirations are subsumed in the desire to produce and consume more and more.

Just as science with humanity is not solely the concern of those who wear white coats and work in laboratories, the ultimate responsibility for commerce with morality does not fall only on multinational corporations or governments. Recently, *Time* magazine, in an editorial that declared Earth the Planet of the Year, said, "No attempt to protect the environment will be successful in the long run unless ordinary people – the California housewife, the Mexican peasant, the Soviet factory worker, the Chinese farmer – are willing to adjust their life-styles. Our wasteful, careless ways must become a thing of the past."

As far as I am concerned, this has the potential to become a very promising situation. If it were up to bureaucracies and boards of directors to determine our fate, it would be far more difficult to change things. But it is not up to them. It is up to us. In matters of commerce and the environment, we are the president, the Supreme Court, and the Congress. *We* decide what to buy and what to ban, what to support and what to discourage.

In other words, the solution is not revolution but evolution. Lasting change happens when people see for themselves that a different way of life is more fulfilling than their present one. This does not happen through government decrees, although they have an important place. To a limited extent, laws do enforce changes, but they rarely inspire people or make them happier. Laws change the way people fulfill their desires, but they cannot show people the beauty of a simpler, more artistic way of life. Only fellow human beings can do that.

My submission is that our image of the human being – of ourselves – influences every aspect of our lives, from politics and economics to education, health care, and relationships. If the quantum theory – a new image of matter and energy – has made revolutionary changes in the sciences, a nobler image of the human being can lead to a much more important evolution in daily living.

The question is, how can this higher image replace the current low image, which is so deeply reinforced by conditioning? How can ordinary people – the California house-wife, the Mexican peasant, the Soviet factory worker, and the Chinese farmer – be inspired to find a new, more efficient way of living, one that is deeply satisfying and joyful yet sensitive to the needs of all?

One thing is certain: nothing will happen if we all wait for others to do it first. The first step in creating a healthy, peaceful postindustrial era is for a few of us to start peeling back the iron mask of conditioning ourselves, basing our lives on a higher image of who we are and a deeper understanding of what we need for a satisfying life. In the midst of a quickly changing world, such "evolutionaries" can provide an inspiring example of what Schumacher calls "a viable future visible in the present": a life built on cooperation, artistry, thrift, and compassion; a life that is not only ecologically sound but vastly more fulfilling than modern industrial life. There may be only a handful of such people to start with, but that should not deter us.

We need men and women who can, as George Bernard Shaw says, dream of things that never were, and ask "Why not?" Our present way of life is characterized by a lack of sensitivity and inventiveness, by a lack of freedom, by hypnotization by the profit motive. We need men and women who can think and invent with a mind filled with compassion, charged with the kind of creativity that finds a place for the smallest songbird and the largest elephant. We need people with the artistry to live in simplicity as the hummingbird does, enjoying the nectar without bruising the flower. We need men and women who delight in working together for a common goal.

This is how we can heal the environment. We have the answer to the environmental crisis already present inside us; it does not have to be invented. But neither do we have to do all the work: biologists tell us there are powerful natural forces that can reverse the damage we have done to the ecosystem. Just as the human body has healing capacities, nature is filled with restorative processes that can heal all the wounds we have inflicted, if we will only give her a chance. Where attempts have been made to reverse environmental illnesses, nature has been quick to respond. It's only when she is overwhelmed by pollution and abuse that she begins to fail.

But I would go much further: we too have great capacities that can be harnessed to restore the environment – restorative powers as great as any found in nature. And we have them in abundant supply: intelligence, discrimination, will, judgment, and – most important – love. Do not underestimate the power of these resources. They too can do much to heal the earth, if we give them a chance.

The Terms of the Trust

Whenever an important decision had to be made in my village, each family was expected to send a representative to take part in the decision-making process. When they had all gathered, the head of the *panchayat* – that was the name of this institution – would stand and give the instructions. His remarks were brief, and whether the decision was about politics or village economics or education or religion, he always said the same thing: "There is only one consideration to take into account. Don't look at this matter from your own point of view. And don't look at it from the way those living in the village now will be affected. Look at it from the point of view of our grandchildren."

That is wonderful advice. Now, when the papers are full of reports on the precarious environmental conditions in which we are forced to live – not by an act of God but by our own consumer frenzy – I think it is time for all of us to ask that question every time we buy something or sell something or pour something down the drain: "How will this affect our grandchildren?"

I was happily reminded of the panchayat recently when I read an article on what is now called sustainable economics. Many modern economists and policymakers are seeking to define and follow a course of sustainable economics as an alternative to what I have called iron mask or consumption-oriented economics. The writer marked a clear contrast between the two: "Traditional economics asks how to produce what for whom. Sustainable economics examines these same questions, but includes future generations in the 'for whom.'"

This is not just advice to the Federal Reserve Board or multinational corporations; it is good advice for all of us. Ordinary people like you and me are the real economists: even though we may not realize it, we all have a choice between iron mask economics and sustainable economics.

How will this affect our grandchildren? Before we buy something that might pollute the environment, before we take an unnecessary trip, before we do anything that might leave the earth a less secure, less green place for our children and grandchildren to grow up in, let us ask that simple question. We are the ones who will decide what kind of earth we leave them. In that sense, we are their trustees, and the first term of the trust is that we are trustees of their environment. It is up to us to see that the environment those children inherit will be at least as healthy as the one we inherited.

As I see it, being a trustee of the environment has two aspects: working in cooperation with nature's restorative processes, and developing the restorative powers within ourselves. These two cannot be separated. We can discover and learn to use the restorative powers of nature – its cooperative principle, its thrift and artistry, its compassion –

only by discovering and using these powers in ourselves. In this process, every crisis becomes an opportunity to learn what nature is teaching us about life and ourselves. It is not so much a duty as an adventure – an adventure in which we discover that, like every other living creature, each of us is a unique and essential member of a compassionate universe.

As my grandmother told me, the elephant does not know how big it is because it looks at the world through such tiny eyes. We too are unaware of our tremendous power to change things. But once we open our eyes to cooperation, artistry, thrift, and compassion, we begin to see thousands of little things we can do to help restore the environment – and restore dignity and deeper fulfillment to our own lives. Each of these things – each "tremendous trifle," to use G. K. Chesterton's lovely phrase – is small by itself but has a broad, beneficial impact. Here are a few suggestions to start with. I am sure you will find plenty of your own.

1. A Reducing Plan

The other day, as I took my morning walk on the beach, I saw what has become a familiar sight on beaches around the world. In the midst of hundreds of "disposable" bottles, utensils, and wrappers left over from a holiday weekend, a seagull was struggling to free its beak from a plastic cup.

I was reminded of a very different scene from my childhood. When my ancestral family held feasts on important holidays, everyone would be served a delectable meal laid out artistically on a banana leaf. When we were finished eating, we gave the leaves as a treat to the cows. Nothing was wasted.

From the standpoint of profit and convenience, plastic packaging has many attractive features: it is strong and light; it is water-resistant; it is inexpensive to produce. But if we looked at plastic from the point of view of our children and grandchildren, we would be hard pressed to find anything of value in it. Its production requires petroleum; it is difficult to recycle; and it often outlives its usefulness, remaining as a nuisance and hazard long after it is thrown away. That morning on the beach, it occurred to me that an appropriate industrial-era blessing might be, "May you last as long as your plastic cup."

One immediate thing we can all do for the environment is look into ways of reducing the amount of garbage we produce, especially items like plastic cups and bottles, batteries, appliances, and household chemicals. Every week, as I mentioned earlier, each of us produces about twenty-five pounds of garbage. Why not just plan to reduce this figure by five pounds? Make it just twenty pounds per week. That will leave a little extra room in the garbage can, and you won't have to take out the trash so often.

This doesn't have to be done overnight. You might start by simply trying to cut back on the amount of packaging you buy. Packaging, I am told, now accounts for one third to one half of our household waste. When you need to buy products packaged in metal or glass, please be sure to recycle. But even better – especially where plastics and toxic chemicals are concerned – *precycle*. "Precycling," a term coined recently, means reducing waste before you buy – by choosing the least-packaged, least-processed product available. Every trip to the grocery store provides dozens of opportunities for precycling.

If these suggestions seem like trifles, remember that they are tremendous trifles. Each time you buy the least-packaged, least-processed product, you are helping to reduce the garbage glut. You are also purifying the atmosphere and saving fossil fuels, since a great deal of oil and coal are used to make the packaging, to process and package

the product, and finally to ship it. And when you buy un-
packaged organic produce, you are giving the small farmer
a much-needed financial boost, since he will be getting a
larger percentage of your purchase. I have nothing against
the people who process and ship food or against big business, but it is up to us as consumers to ensure a place for
small business as well. Let us see that the small farmer,
who farms organically and with an eye toward conserv-
ing the soil and water, flourishes.

To me, cutting down on waste is a fine example of com-
bining thrift and cooperation to make daily life a work of
art. In every form of art, from painting to architecture to
poetry, isn't it considered the height of taste to leave nothing superfluous, to use every element of the composition
in the most elegant and efficient manner? By this standard, what could be more beautiful than a meal that comes
straight from the farm, or from your own garden? I go to
the theater regularly and enjoy concerts and dances, but
I can think of nothing more utterly artistic than such a
meal. Not only is it fresh, tasty, nourishing, and free
of toxic residues, but it is a living expression of love for
Mother Earth. This is postindustrial art at its highest.

As I said, it does not have to happen overnight. Once
you get the hang of it, next Christmas you can say to your
neighbor, "Hey, Julie, let's make it fifteen pounds of garbage a week." That is a fine Christmas present; it is inexpensive and very healthy for your children. If cooperation
doesn't work, you can even try competition: "Julie, this
year I'm giving you the finest Christmas present you will
ever get – ten pounds less garbage a week. It is going to
benefit your children as well as mine." One day, Julie will
say to her husband, "Maybe this isn't such a bad idea. After
all, it doesn't cost anything. Why don't *we* go for eleven?"
Slowly but surely, each one of us can generate only a third

of a ton of garbage a year, then a quarter, then – who knows? – maybe just some compost.

2. *The Breath of Life*

To start healing the atmosphere, we do not need to make drastic changes, or even dramatic ones. We can all start small.

Recently the city of Berkeley, responding to reports of a link between the chlorofluorocarbons used in many foam containers and the depletion of the ozone layer, passed a measure banning the use of polystyrene plastic for fast foods or other foods packaged by local retailers. I no longer live in Berkeley, but I too have banned polystyrene packaging. Wherever I go I take my own cup along, and when I get a decaf capuccino to go, I hand the waitress my cup. This usually provokes some curiosity: "Why do you carry that cup around with you?" I enjoy telling people, "I carry it because I love children and the earth. Every time I use it I am preserving millions of ozone molecules."

People are not unkind; no one wants to hurt the environment. Often we just cannot see the connections. Taking my cup along is my way of gently saying, "Do you have any children or grandchildren? Do you love them? Then get a cup like this." Wherever you go, wherever you work, you can take this simple, artistic step, which hurts no one, requires no extra time or money, and helps people see the beauty of loving Mother Earth.

Similarly, to counteract the greenhouse effect, we do not have to renounce fossil fuels. There is a reasonable margin for their use, since Mother Earth provides an abundance of trees to "breathe" in our carbon dioxide and return oxygen. But all of us, as an expression of love for our grandchildren and for the earth, can look for ways to produce less carbon dioxide.

If we are to stabilize our climate, experts think that we must reduce by one half the amount of carbon dioxide we release through fossil fuel combustion. Each mile you fly in an airplane, you are responsible for generating about one-half pound of carbon dioxide. Each kilowatt-hour of electricity from a coal-fired power plant produces two pounds of carbon dioxide. For each gallon of gas you burn in your car you are responsible for twenty pounds of carbon dioxide.

Another gift, then, that you can give the children is to try to depend on these things a little less. We need not be unrealistic: there are occasions when we need to travel by airplane, but let's try to do it only when necessary. And we often need to use our cars – then we can express our love by taking a few people along. Try to rearrange your schedule so you can start early and go a little out of your way to pick up a friend. This will not always be easy, but every time you travel with two people per car instead of one, you are cutting your personal pollution by fifty percent. Before long, if we all do this, a quiet revolution will begin to take place: traffic and accidents will be reduced by fifty percent, and the children's lives will be enriched by a hundred percent.

The more loving people may want to say, "We'll take three." (Such people also get past the toll gate free.) Passionately loving people will say, "We'll take five." The air will become cleaner and cleaner; and the people in those cars will not be isolated, lonely commuters – they can talk, smile at each other, be together.

I am also not against buying new cars when necessary. But I would say, when you buy a new car, plant a dozen trees around the garage. In fact, if I were the president of General Motors, I would insist on it: "Have you planted your trees, Gerard? If so, you may have your car. If not, go plant them and then come back."

Each tree we plant is, in the language of Madison Avenue, a gift that keeps on giving. Every day of the year it takes in our carbon dioxide and gives us back oxygen. Indeed, according to a recent article by James R. Udall, "a fast-growing tree can 'fix' as much as forty-eight pounds of carbon dioxide each year. A tree's ability to shade buildings, particularly in urban concrete jungles, can save fifteen times that amount indirectly in avoided energy costs."

The American Forestry Association – whose motto is "plant a tree, cool the globe" – says there are about one hundred million spaces to plant trees around our homes and communities. So instead of buying things that are neither necessary nor beneficial, let us buy things that are both: tree seedlings. Each one costs as little as a dollar. Planting twelve trees would take just three or four hours, and it is something family and friends can do together. A dozen trees planted by every family would do a great deal to ensure that our grandchildren have pure air.

You may notice that these simple measures solve one problem by solving another. When working in the garden, for example, you are saving fossil fuel, reducing garbage, preserving the health of the topsoil, and decreasing carbon dioxide emissions – all at once, while you have a nice afternoon with the children. When you buy local produce and crafts and support locally owned restaurants, barbershops, and drugstores, you are saving fossil fuels and helping others to make a healthful, satisfying living by owning their own business. The sense of community this builds makes shopping more pleasant and enourages trusting relationships – and gives you a say in which products are sold.

This is a very different approach from the industrial one, in which we usually solve one problem by creating several more. We deal with a traffic problem by building more freeways and bridges. Soon there are more cars to fill up those freeways; then we spend millions of dollars to add more lanes, all the while ignoring the real problem: a way of life based on unlimited consumption in a world of limited resources.

Let me repeat: I am not one of those who say, "Let's go back five thousand years and live as our ancestors did." Not at all. There is wide provision in nature for the efficient, cooperative use of cars, for the artistic, thrifty use of technology, for compassionate commerce. But let us keep our sense of perspective. When someone proposes to make your home town a world-class city by adding four lanes to the freeway or by drilling oil wells off the coast, please take the time to stand up and ask, "How will this affect our grandchildren?"

3. A Compassionate Diet

As you learn to see yourself as a trustee for your children's planet and gradually let thrift and cooperation shape your life, you will begin to see that all our environmental problems are actually messages from a compassionate Mother Earth. She is trying to remind us that we have overlooked our deepest sources of abiding joy and fulfillment.

Consider, for instance, the destruction of the tropical rain forest, much of which is being burned to make way for cattle ranches. The beef from these ranches goes to the wealthy industrialized nations of the West – and now Japan as well. I heard recently about a group that has begun boycotting certain food chains that have a vested interest in these cattle ranches. I too am eager to see this destruction stop, but my suggestion is different. To me, it is all so simple. There is no need to boycott; just make use of your innate capacity for compassion by becoming a vegetarian.

By reducing the demand for beef, each vegetarian saves one acre of rain forest a year. At present, there are about ten million vegetarians in the United States. Now that nutritionists and health care professionals are beginning to recommend a vegetarian diet, we may well have a hundred million vegetarians in this country by the end of the century. If we can do that, we will have saved a great part of the Central and South American rain forest.

We do not have to become ascetics; vegetarian cuisine is thoroughly delicious and satisfying. Let us just make sure that the food we prepare at home and ask for in restaurants satisfies not only our palate but the needs of Mother Earth. If we could learn the language of compassion, we would hear her say, "Treat all living creatures with care and respect. There will be clean air and fresh rain for everyone. There will be forests to explore, where you will find medicines to help keep you healthy. Together we will thrive." This is how the compassionate universe works: we enrich ourselves by enriching nature; nature enriches herself by enriching us.

Minimum Means, Maximum Joy

Trusteeship as a way of life is an artistic combination of great comfort and great simplicity: using minimum means to achieve maximum joy, without ever hurting nature. The personal benefits are enormous. When you spend less money on unnecessary things, you don't need to spend so much time working to pay for them. You can slow down a little. You have time to go to the beach with your children and bask in the beauty of the sea, to listen to the birds and admire the sunset, to watch the stars appear in the evening sky.

I am not speaking theoretically. A group of friends and I have been doing our best to live this way for the past twenty years. We all lead active lives, some holding jobs as doctors or teachers or carpenters or artists, others raising families, and all of us enjoying the benefits of modern life. We have found that changes like these bring us together as friends and make us healthier and more secure, knowing we are helping to make the earth a little greener for all children to grow up in.

The lesson of the hummingbird is that beauty and nobility are to be found not in having more but in having just what is necessary. I always make it clear that I am no fan of poverty; I don't think anyone anywhere should live in poverty. But isn't it a little vulgar to pile up material possessions as an indication of our own worth when more than half the world lives in aching need – and when the very production of those things often harms the environment for our own children?

To be trustees, there is no need to live in misery or to give up the things we need for a long, healthy, enjoyable life. Nobody need deprive himself or herself of legitimate comforts, of equipment for work, of attractive clothing or good schools or healthy entertainment. Let's simply post a question mark on the door of the mind, addressed to every desire that requests entrance: "Halt! Who goes there? Are you a friend to all of life? Do you contribute to my health and the health of all creatures? If so, you may pass. If you injure me or those around me, even if you are tasty or tempting, go knocking elsewhere. You will find no welcome here."

Regardless of what Madison Avenue tells us, our real hunger is not for things but for a higher image of ourselves. No amount of material possessions will ever make us secure or fulfilled.

The practical suggestions in this chapter are a few first steps all of us can take right away. They will help the environment, and they will help us discover just a little more of our own capacity for cooperation, thrift, artistry, and compassion. In scientific terms, they are a way to start testing the hypothesis of a compassionate universe.

Nevertheless, it is important to be realistic: the conditioning that has caused such damage to our environment and made the world such a dangerous place will not disappear just because a few of us start planting trees or using our cars less. It will take a long battle to triumph over our conditioning. I am firmly convinced, however, that it is a battle we can win.

The program of trusteeship I present in the next three chapters takes environmentalism a step further than it is usually taken, into the place where our environmental problems begin: the mind. That is where the real fight for the future of the earth will be waged. The environmental crisis is not a separate, isolated concern. It is connected with all our attitudes, conscious and unconscious: toward each other, toward other countries, toward our children, toward ourselves. Until these attitudes change, we will go on damaging the environment, no matter what sort of surface changes we make.

Of course, this is not going to be easy, and the first steps will be among the most difficult. It is rather like using muscles you have not used for a long time; you need to build a bridge between your knowledge and your will, and that is sheer exertion. Yet those first steps are also exhilarating. The moment we look beyond our own small satisfactions, we begin to see a whole new world, filled with opportunities.

I remember watching my friends' little girl, Christina, take her first steps. For a few months, I had seen her crawling – or "swimming," as we say in India – around my study. Her style was eclectic, a kind of Australian crawl, and to look at her it was hard to imagine that the thought of walking would ever cross her mind.

Then one day I was working in my study with Christina sitting on the floor near me. Suddenly the world seemed to hold its breath: slowly, little by little by little, she began to pull herself up. It was poetry in motion; even the deer and birds outside the window seemed to wait and watch. But it was also solid science: unable to stand on her own power, she used my chair as support; and she didn't keep her feet close together but placed them wide apart to keep her center of gravity close to the ground. Finally, standing bravely on her own, she looked at me with such a triumphant smile that I applauded. As the years passed, she has learned to walk, to jog, to run, to play tag; I doubt if she can remember a time when she couldn't walk.

Like Christina, all of us have passed through a time when, if we had been asked to walk, we would have been utterly bewildered. "Walking? What is this walking? I'll just lie here and wait for Mommy to do everything for me – pick me up, feed me, carry me – that's what life is for."

And yet, even as she crawled about, Christina had been watching me carefully. In her subconscious the desire to stand up was waiting in the wings, whispering with mounting impatience, "Just a little longer . . . just a few more months, and I too will be striding around the study."

If we listen carefully, we can hear a quiet voice inside asking, "Is this all there is to life? Are we human beings so weak and insecure that we must content ourselves with Cadillacs and cigarettes while the world falls apart? Are we so limited in our understanding of each other that we must fight over profits and ideology while children starve and the earth is destroyed?" Anyone who can muster the daring and perseverance to listen to this inner voice, and follow its call to the core of personality, will testify that the stature of the human being is so sublime that we will remain hungry and thirsty until everyone learns to live in freedom.

Because we have not taken the time to look past our conditioning, we see ourselves as a few dollars' worth of chemicals, driven to compete with one another and exhaust our earth. How could anyone be taken in by such a mediocre portrait of human nature? Believing that this is who we are, we have let ourselves be so hypnotized by the desire for profit and pleasure and power that we now seem practically helpless before the forces that are greedily devouring the earth.

But this is only a case of mistaken identity. Scratch the portrait's surface and something altogether different begins to shine through: a much different image of who we are.

According to the industrial hypothesis, we are insignificant specks who can find fulfillment, or consolation for the lack of it, only in having more and more things. In the industrial context, competition for resources has provided the only legitimate motivation for human conduct.

The alternative hypothesis is far from new. It was enunciated three thousand years ago in the Gita, and it can be found at the core of each of the world's great religious traditions: in every one of us, beneath the surface level of conditioned thinking, there is a single living spirit. The still, small voice whispering to me in the depths of my consciousness is saying exactly the same thing as the voice whispering to you: "I want an earth that is healthy, a world at peace, and a heart filled with love." It doesn't matter if your skin is brown or white or black or whether you speak English, Japanese, or Malayalam – the voice, says the Gita, is the same in every creature, and it comes from your true self.

Again, I do not offer this as a dogma or a tenet of faith. It is a scientific hypothesis that can be tested by anyone with

the daring and determination needed to pursue the course
of investigation. Nor is it an intellectual theory. It is an experience that revolutionizes the individual's perception of
the universe and brings profound changes in character, conduct, and consciousness – changes that leave their mark on
everything he or she does, and deeply influence everyone
he or she comes in contact with.

The practical, day-to-day implications are enormous.
A trustee lives according to the realization that the world
is home to billions of living creatures, all of whom have an
equal right to a healthy environment and a life in peace. A
trustee understands that human beings – the most powerful
creatures on earth – are meant to find happiness not in ex-
ploiting or manipulating their fellow creatures but in protecting them and enriching their environment.

In this way, trusteeship is exactly the opposite of the
industrial hypothesis, which looks on our earth and resources as a kind of treasure chest to be plundered by the
most cunning or powerful. To the trustee, the earth –
Mother Earth – is a beloved friend. His abiding desire is to
adorn her with all the things she loves: trees, clean water, a
rich topsoil, and all she needs for countless generations of
healthy, secure children. Such a person stands at the crown
of life, a protector and safe refuge for all that lives. Is there
a nobler goal for humanity to strive for?

There is surely none more challenging. The sages of
ancient India compare such a way of life to walking the
edge of a razor, and from my own small experience I can
attest that they were not exaggerating. Self-transformation
is a long, slow process, requiring patience and determination, but there is no human being who is not capable of it.

The next three chapters will explore a practical method I
have developed to incorporate cooperation, artistry, thrift,
and compassion into every aspect of contemporary life. It is

a program of trusteeship designed to be used by anyone, regardless of race or religion, who wants to find personal fulfillment and live in a healthier world.

When a person takes up this challenge in earnest, it is only a matter of time before an ever-increasing circle of people see the beauty and common sense of such a life. We are entering a period of great change; people are beginning to see the limits of the industrial hypothesis, yet they have nothing to replace it. Again, as Beveridge remarks, "It is easier to drop the old hypothesis if one can find a new one to replace it. The feeling of disappointment too will then vanish." When we live as trustees, we are offering that new hypothesis to everyone we come in contact with.

In this way, we can slowly but surely lead the world back to health. It is we – not governments or corporations but ordinary people like you and me – who can ensure that the twentieth century will be remembered not as the nuclear age, or as the last century of a habitable earth, but as the beginning of a postindustrial era, an age of compassion.

We need people in every field who can serve as a bridge between humanity and its highest aspirations. We need mothers who dream of their children growing up in a compassionate society and ask: *why not?* We need scientists, businesspeople, politicians, and journalists who have the courage to dream of a world where people, animals, and the environment are more important than profits or national rivalries and ask: *why not?* We need ordinary people of every nation and color who dare to look beneath the iron mask of conditioning, see something they never believed they could be, and ask themselves: *why not?*

Part Three / Trusteeship of Ourselves
and the Earth

*The tasks facing us today are
enormous, but it is the glory of
human nature that there will
always be those rare individuals
who say, "Let there be dangers,
let there be difficulties – whatever
it costs, I want to live to the full
height of my being, my feet still
on the ground but my head crowned
with stars." According to Mahatma
Gandhi, this can be done only by
facing difficulties that appear almost
impossible. If that is so, the 1990s
offer an unparalleled opportunity.*

An Instrument of Peace

Since war begins in the minds of men, it is in the minds of men that the defenses of peace must be constructed.
—*UNESCO Charter*

I have learnt through bitter experience the one supreme lesson to conserve my anger, and as heat conserved is transmuted into energy, even so our anger controlled can be transmuted into a power which can move the world.
—*Mahatma Gandhi*

In one of my favorite Sanskrit stories from ancient India, an ambitious rat goes to the Lord and asks to become a human being. The Lord grants his wish, and the rat is born into the world of people. He spends several lifetimes as a human being; finally, after quite a bit of experimentation and a great deal of grief, he goes back to the Lord and implores, "Please make me a rat again. Being a human is too hard – I'm just not cut out for it."

I often think of this story when people tell me I am being idealistic about human nature. "It would be nice," they say, "if we human beings could override impulses like fear, greed, and violence when we see that they threaten the welfare of the whole. But that's just not realistic. Whenever there is a conflict between reason and biology, biology is bound to win."

Arguing like this, some observers feel that we have passed the point of no return. Like lemmings, they seem to say, we must race to a destruction we ourselves shall have caused. I differ categorically. Whatever we feel we know about animals – and I suspect there is a good deal still to be learned – no observation about animal behavior need hold true for a human being.

In me, in you – in every human being – burns a spark of pure compassion: not physical or even mental, but deeply spiritual. Our bodies may belong to the animal world, but *we* do not. The animal, to a great extent, lives subject to the force of conditioning, going after its own food and comfort. But we have the capacity to turn our back on profit or pleasure for the sake of others – to rebel deeply and broadly against our conditioning and to build a new personality, a new world. It is our choice whether to exercise that capacity, but we have the choice.

When I taught in Berkeley during the sixties, I often

reminded my students that, no matter what they heard to the contrary, they were not rats or mice or guinea pigs.

As far as I am concerned, the distinguishing feature of the human being is neither opposable thumbs nor the capacity to speak the Queen's English; it is the ability to live by the law of unity, to live for the benefit of all life. The human being can always choose to act as a trustee for the environment, to go without a few material advantages in order to alleviate the suffering of others. Our glory is the capacity to leave self-interest behind.

As Gandhi once said, the dignity of man requires obedience to a higher law. It is this higher law of unity that we have omitted – albeit with a few shining exceptions – from our political life. It does not even figure in our deliberations on the most important issues. Politics without principles, in Gandhi's perspective, is politics in service of our lowest and least human faculties. Examples are easy to find.

The so-called balance of power, for instance, bears more resemblance to a balance of terror, in which each superpower vies with the other in devising weapons, and then sells them wholesale to developing countries. We are conditioned to believe that suspicion, secrecy, and self-interest form the only possible foundation for foreign policy. This conditioning runs so deep that many people have trouble believing anything else could work. For that reason, it may be helpful to describe a leader who turned his back on self-interest – and flourished.

In the third century B.C., Prince Ashoka was born into a dynasty of great warriors – his grandfather had driven out the garrison established in northwest India by Alexander the Great. Ashoka ascended the throne in 268 B.C., inheriting an empire that extended from what is now central India up into central Asia. Empires never seem to be big enough, however, and nine years into his reign Ashoka launched a massive campaign to win the rest of the subcontinent.

The land of Kalinga lay immediately to the south. Despite fierce resistance, it was finally subdued. Victorious, young Emperor Ashoka was at the height of his power. The rest of the subcontinent would be easy prey; it was now within his grasp to rule the largest empire in Asia. But as Ashoka walked that day on the battlefield of Kalinga, his troops shouting and singing in celebration, a tremendous change took place deep in his consciousness. At the sight of the battlefield, littered with the dead and maimed bodies of other young men like himself, he was so stricken by the human cost of war that he immediately ceased his campaign, renounced violence entirely, and devoted the rest of his reign to serving the welfare of his people.

This story appealed deeply to my students in Berkeley, who were troubled by the war then being waged in Vietnam. I am pleased to say that it was young people like them across the country who, more than anyone else, opened the eyes of the nation to the horror and futility of war.

Terrible as the Vietnam War was – and grave as the specter of the arms race and nuclear proliferation in the Third World are – we are faced with a far more deadly and consuming threat today: the prospect of a burnt-out, wasted environment. We are at war with our own future, colonized not by some other nation or race, but by our own unintended greed.

"Hatred does not cease by hatred," said the Compassionate Buddha just three centuries before Ashoka walked the battlefield of Kalinga. "Hatred ceases by love alone." Surely those words must have echoed in the consciousness of young Emperor Ashoka that day. It was not long before he had made peace with the southern region of India, retreating from its borders and giving it protection.

Ashoka became a follower of the Compassionate Buddha and transformed his life into a model of trusteeship. He lived, according to the Buddha's words, "for the happiness of all, for the welfare of all." He built roads throughout his kingdom, with way stations for travelers; he planted thousands of trees and established universities and monasteries. He built hospitals for people and for animals. He made laws that are still exemplary for their humanity, and he established a state policy of mutual respect for all religions. His foreign policy, even toward traditional enemies, was based on friendship; free trade and cultural exchange were encouraged with all countries.

For the thirty remaining years of Ashoka's reign, he maintained friendly relations with surrounding nations. His people prospered; trade and culture flourished. In relating his horror after the conquest of Kalinga, Ashoka commented – the words are almost the Buddha's own – that no one can truly be conquered except by love; and he added, in a new kind of royal pride, that he had already made many such conquests, not only in his own kingdom but in other lands as well.

"Amidst the tens of thousands of names of monarchs that crowd the columns of history," wrote H. G. Wells, "the name of Ashoka shines, and shines almost alone, a star. From the Volga to Japan his name is still honoured. . . . More living men cherish his memory today than have ever heard the names of Constantine or Charlemagne."

We might be tempted to think, "If only we had such a leader today . . ." But today it is not monarchs or even politicians who wage war. A leader like Ashoka would be only a beginning. In the words of the UNESCO charter, "war begins in the minds of men" – not just in the minds of politicians, but in the minds of every one of us. It is we ordinary people who are waging war on the earth and each other at this very moment – through the corporations and institutions we support with our purchases, through our wasteful life-style, but most of all through our inability to break the chains of conditioned self-interest.

Helplessness runs against the grain of the human being. We are not rats. We are born not to be helpless but to fight – to fight until we triumph. Think of the courage, the strength, the fierce desire to succeed that have marked humanity's greatest achievements. These are among our most precious resources: we have simply turned them against the wrong enemy.

My grandmother was born into the *kshatriya* caste – the caste that provided ancient India's fiercest warriors. She often reminded me of the distinguishing mark of a kshatriya: no matter how desperate the battle, there will be no wounds on his back. She taught me that every human being is born to fight like this, with the utmost courage and endurance; yet she never neglected to add that when we fight others we always lose. When the smoke clears, she would say, we will have lost a potential friend and gained an enemy. But each time we fight against the forces that hold us down and keep us from loving, we draw a little closer to the rest of life.

The terrorism that has become almost commonplace in many parts of the Third World should be proof enough that when we battle others – whether for pride or profit or pos- sessions – all we win are enemies. Happiness built on the suffering of others will not last long; when our power fades, as it eventually must, we reap a bitter harvest of ill will, resentment, and revenge.

But when the battle is waged within, against the forces of anger and selfishness we find in our own hearts, even our smallest triumph benefits the whole world. The energy, courage, and clarity released make us a dynamic force for good: the power of such a person is not divided by five billion competitors but multiplied by five billion friends.

Europe's Greatest Environmentalist

That course I taught at Berkeley – Religious Studies 138X, four units' credit – was a course in rebellion. Not the placard-waving, window-breaking type of rebellion, but a far more potent and effective one: rebellion against conditioning. The method: a systematic training of the mind called meditation.

The program of trusteeship I will outline in the final section of this book is essentially a tool for training the mind. It is a series of dynamic disciplines that, if pursued systematically and with sustained enthusiasm, will enable you to build a steady and reliable bridge between your knowledge and your will. In scientific terms, it is an experiment – by the mind, with the mind, and on the mind – through which you can acquire the capacity to decide the course of your thoughts and actions instead of letting them be determined by your conditioning. It contains nothing I have not tested exhaustively and found successful in my own life, while leading a very active career on university campuses in India and America.

I have published a complete guide to this eight-point program in my book *Meditation*. Here I will present selected aspects of the program and suggest how they may be used in healing the environment. At the heart of the program is meditation: half an hour every morning, as early as is convenient. The form of meditation I recommend has been adapted from the world's major mystical traditions – Hindu, Buddhist, Christian, Islamic – for use in an active, modern context.

The instructions can be given in a paragraph. Find a clean, peaceful place. Sit in a straight-backed chair or on the floor, and gently close your eyes. Then begin to go slowly, in your mind, through one of the passages from the scriptures or the great mystics that are appropriate for use in meditation. (I will explain this more fully below.) Do not follow any association of ideas or think about the passage; if you are giving your full attention to each word, the meaning cannot help sinking in. When distractions come, do not resist them, but give more attention to the words of the passage. If your mind strays from the passage entirely, bring it back gently to the beginning and start again.

The principle of meditation can be given in a phrase: we become what we meditate on – in the words of the Buddha, "we become what we think." The things we think about, brood on, dwell on, and exult over influence our life in a thousand different ways. When we can actually choose the direction of our thoughts instead of just letting them run along the grooves of conditioned thinking, we become the masters of our own lives. Obviously, the kind of passage you meditate on is a matter of great importance. It is vital to choose a passage that is both positive and practical. On the one hand, it should embody your highest goals and inspire you with the noblest image of yourself; on the other, it should lead you into the rich challenges of daily life, where you will be able to make use of the tremendous resources released by deepening meditation.

When I began teaching meditation in the United States, I looked for a passage that contained the very best of the West's great tradition of wisdom and practicality. My search ended when I discovered a short passage by an extraordinary ordinary man, whom I often described to my students.

As far as I am concerned, he was the greatest environmentalist, peacemaker, and rebel in European history. At a time when Europe had lost direction, he presented an alternative, which has influenced millions of people down to the present century. Rather than diminish the effect of his life, passing centuries have only enhanced it. In fact, along with cultural, religious, and political leaders from around the world, the World Wildlife Fund cosponsored a celebration of the eight hundredth anniversary of his birth. The ceremony took place in the small Italian town where he was born and grew up, Assisi.

I often recognize the young Francis Bernardone in the young people of America: idealistic, friendly, energetic, and full of high spirits, but lacking in direction. Francis was an excellent salesman, whose charm and good manners brought the wealthiest clientele to his father's fabric shop; even as a young man, he was assured of a comfortable middle-class living at a time when this could not be taken for granted. Yet Francis was not satisfied with shopkeeping. He liked to think of himself as a troubador; today, I suppose, he might fancy himself a singer in a band. I can easily picture him with a guitar: the life of the party, a young man with grand but vaguely defined ambitions. At one point, attracted by popular stories of chivalry, Francis even donned a suit of armor and rode off to fight against a neighboring city.

But then, in one of history's most remarkable transformations, this fashionable but somewhat ordinary young man, who had been drifting so pleasantly and ineffectively through his youth, did a sharp U-turn. To change metaphors, you might say he began to swim upstream, against the current of his conditioning, changing his every response, motivation, and ambition. For a brief, shining moment, Francis had caught a glimpse of the radiant figure at the core of the human personality, and he dedicated the rest of his life to molding himself to that image as closely as he could.

I would say that Francis did not give up music but learned to play a much more subtle music, which is as beautiful and as audible today as it was seven hundred years ago. He discovered a source of energy, wisdom, and strength within his own heart that set the hearts of millions of people on fire with the desire for peace and brotherhood. Even today, the mention of his name is enough to invoke a spirit of reverence for nature and the hope that true peace is possible – even in the twentieth century – among people of every country, religion, and color.

Few people are not drawn by Francis's simple joy in loving others, yet it is not always easy to see how we can relate to this figure from the Middle Ages, the "poor little man of Assisi." As my students used to ask me: in an age of sixty thousand nuclear weapons, of television, plastics, and the automobile, what is the "relevance" of this one man, born eight hundred years ago?

If you want to understand Francis's power, I would answer, don't look in history books; and you needn't go to Assisi or learn Italian or study ancient manuscripts. His secret lies not in history but in the present. It lies, in fact, deep within your own heart and mind. The source of Francis's tremendous impact was nothing other than his unswerving loyalty to the still, small voice within him – the same voice that is at this moment speaking in the depths of your own consciousness.

And Francis, eager to share the source of his love and creativity with all of humanity, left a map by which others may find their way. Or, if you like, consider it a musical score: his most subtle and powerful composition, which you can learn to play with the instrument of your life.

Lord, make me an instrument of thy peace.
Where there is hatred, let me sow love;
Where there is injury, pardon;
Where there is doubt, faith;
Where there is despair, hope;
Where there is darkness, light;
Where there is sadness, joy.

O divine Master, grant that I may not so much seek
To be consoled as to console,
To be understood as to understand,
To be loved as to love;
For it is in giving that we receive;
It is in pardoning that we are pardoned;
It is in dying [to self] that we are born to eternal life.

In this and the following chapters I will comment on
this passage, line by line, to draw out some of its practical
implications for the life of a trustee.

Transformation

Lord, make me an instrument of thy peace.

Let us start with the first word, "Lord." It is important to
understand that Francis is not asking to become an instrument in the hands of some white-bearded figure seated on a
throne between the Milky Way and Andromeda galaxies.
He is turning inward. Similarly, when we meditate on this
passage, we are not speaking to someone else. We are direct-
ing a call to the depths of our unconscious, asking our own
deepest self – who lives there unsuspected and unhonored
– to make us a blessing to all those we come in contact
with. Help me change my life, we are asking; give me

clearer eyes; let the thick fog of conditioning clear enough that I can see how to serve humanity.

To find your real self, say the mystics of every religious tradition, look inside – at your deepest resources of love, compassion, and wisdom. Through the practice of meditation you will uncover a figure that outshines your present self-image a millionfold. In my presentation, the aspiration of a trustee is to search for, discover, and serve that spirit, which is alive in the heart of every creature.

Francis's lovely phrase, an instrument of peace, is a perfect description of any man or woman who nourishes that aspiration. When Francis says "peace," he is not just referring to an absence of war. As the Dutch philosopher Spinoza says, peace "is a virtue, a state of mind, a disposition for benevolence, confidence, and justice." Wherever a trustee goes, he or she tries to bring along that state of mind, inspiring and supporting others as they struggle to live up to their highest ideals.

Some people find it hard to believe they can ever become such a person. Our conditioning tells us that we are born with a particular disposition and that, although we can make small, superficial changes in our personality, we actually have little choice in how we respond to life. The universal claim of the mystics, to which I can add my own testimony based on personal experience, is that it is possible to remake our personality entirely, according to our own chosen specifications; we can become completely independent of our conditioning.

This is not an ethical or moral presentation but a dynamic one. Trusteeship, as I present it, is a process of investigation and transformation. On the one hand, you turn inward to find a higher image of yourself; on the other, you use that image to transform every aspect of your life.

Like a sculptor, you set your ideal on your mental easel each morning in meditation, look as clearly at it as you can, and then carry that inspiration with you into the day to chip away all that is not your true self.

The best way to learn about meditation is to try it yourself. To start with, though, I can give you a little idea of what happens in meditation and why it is such a powerful tool for self-transformation.

The challenge begins with the very first line. You have closed your eyes and begun repeating the words silently in your mind, as slowly as possible: "Lord . . . make me . . ." So far, so good. Your mind is focused on the words, you are attentive and alert; but before long you notice that a distraction has popped by to say hello: "What shall we have for breakfast this morning?" By himself he seems harmless, so you invite him in and answer, "Belgian waffles." Unfortunately, as he enters he leaves the door open behind him, and his friends crowd in to check out the scene. One after another, and sometimes all at once, they raise their voices: "What tie shall we wear today? Who won the ball game yesterday? I wish I didn't have to go to work." Before long, you have lost the passage. Perhaps your mind has even left with one of the more attractive thoughts for champagne brunch at a fashionable restaurant. So you take your mind back to the beginning of the passage and start again. This time, you resolve, it will be different. But your mind is not listening to you. It does not leave completely this time, but the words are coming out quite strangely: "Lord . . . make me . . . a cup of tea . . ."

At this point it is not unusual to wonder, as the Catholic mystic Augustine did, just what is going on. "I can tell my hand what to do," he exclaimed once; "why can't I tell my mind what to do?" With one voice, the mystics of every country respond: don't blame your mind; you just haven't yet trained it to do what you want it to.

When you first begin to meditate, your mind may be distracted thirty or forty times in half an hour. After a few years of sustained, enthusiastic practice – the kind of practice that goes into making a great swimmer or musician or mountain climber – perhaps it will wander just ten times; after five years, just four or five times. Eventually it is possible to train your mind to rest completely on the passage.

What is happening is that gradually, day by day, you are acquiring the ability to tell your mind what to think. You are teaching it to rest in the state of mind which Spinoza described as benevolent, confident, and just – regardless of any misfortunes or challenges that may come your way. That is the greatest freedom we can hope for; it means we are gaining control of our lives at the deepest level of consciousness. With that control comes the skill to shape our entire life into an instrument of peaceful change – in our home, our community, our nation, our world.

A Bear in a Cage

> Where there is hatred, let me sow love;
> Where there is injury, pardon;
> Where there is doubt, faith.

Coming from the Third World, I have often made the plea to Third World audiences, "Don't dwell on past injustices. Don't bear grudges from the record of colonialism. Those centuries are over, passed into the dustbin of history. As Gandhi would have said, an eye for an eye only makes the whole world blind. Why not begin afresh?"

I think many of our troubles, from personal quarrels to global conflicts, can be attributed to our inability to put aside resentments about the past and focus with clarity and common sense on the problem at hand. The Treaty of Versailles, for instance, did little to heal the wounds of World War I and actually sowed the seeds of World War II. If you look at the conclusion of World War II you can see the shape of coming events, as it casts a dark shadow into the future. But, in international affairs as in individual relationships, when we slip and offend one another or say thoughtless things, it helps to remember that making mistakes is all part of living and learning. Meditation can give us the capacity to learn from those mistakes and to put them behind us.

By restoring our sovereignty over the thinking process, meditation helps us develop the precious skill of starting afresh. Ordinarily, a great deal of our mental energy is focused on the past, on what others have done to us or what we have done to them. Because so much of our attention is absorbed in these fruitless preoccupations, we are often unable to see promising opportunities right in front of us.

Quite often, a person's hostile attitude toward us has little to do with us. That person may be feeling insecure or frightened, and because we too feel insecure or suspicious, we misinterpret the signals and assume he wishes us ill. We get angry, he gets angrier, and the vicious circle begins. Many superpower conflicts are nothing more than this childish misery-go-round: you expelled my ambassador, so I'll expel yours; you are pointing missiles at me, so I'll point missiles at you.

When we learn to slow down the thinking process, we acquire the distinctly human ability to separate stimulus from response. We begin to see that in every situation, we have a choice. To paraphrase the Buddha, when someone tries to offend us, we can say to ourselves, "If you are angry at me, why should I be angry at you? What is the connection?" With this detachment comes the freedom to choose a response that helps solve the problem rather than compound it. We can walk into the most tense, antagonistic situation with a mind calm and relaxed, and help create a harmonious, creative dialogue – between people, between groups, even between nations.

Anyone who develops this skill, as Gandhi did, gains the power to transform his most impassioned enemies into friends. Carrying this to the national level, we can replace a first-strike capacity with a first-trust capacity. If a nation expels our ambassador, we can invite ten more of its ambassadors and have a good discussion of our common interests. Even if a country were to close its borders to our people, we could send a few of our friendliest dogs on an exchange program to help its people remember that their dogs are no different from ours. Slowly, the dogs would help us all remember that we too are the same. In other words, instead of being caught in a vicious circle, we can start a virtuous circle – not by closing our eyes to hostility or capitulating to it, but by remaining secure even under attack, and by recognizing that the real opponent is not the other person or the other nation but the conditioning that has convinced us we are enemies.

The key to this process is the ability to harness our anger. I do not mean suppressing or repressing anger, nor do I mean releasing anger in the way so often advocated in recent years. I am referring to a third alternative, little understood in the modern world: the deliberate harnessing of anger as a powerful force for change.

Gandhi once wrote, "I have learnt through bitter experience the one supreme lesson to conserve my anger, and as heat conserved is transmuted into energy, even so our anger controlled can be transmuted into a power which can

Chapter Six

move the world." Anger, like electricity, is a powerful
force. We all know that electricity unharnessed can destroy
life; but safely and skillfully directed, it gives us light and
heat. The same is true of anger: it can destroy us, or – if we
can learn to harness its tremendous energy – it can light up
the world with love, forgiveness, and faith. This is the practical meaning of Francis's lines, "Where there is hatred, let
me sow love; where there is injury, pardon; where there is
doubt, faith."

These are not abstract ideas; they are living realities that
we can draw on in any situation. Perhaps I can illustrate
with one or two small events from my own life. The first
occurred when my wife and I were living on the Blue Mountain in India. One afternoon, we went to visit a friend on
the other side of town. As we walked through the bazaar
on the way to his place, we saw a large, noisy crowd mill-
ing about. In the center of the crowd stood an awkward,
poorly built cage with a thoroughly miserable bear slumped
on the floor. His coat was mangy; he seemed not to have
eaten for days; and there was so little room in the cage that
he could barely turn around. The bear's owner was circulating among the onlookers, collecting money.

Deeply disturbed, we walked on to our friend's house
and took him back with us to see the bear. He was a kind
man, always sensitive to the suffering of animals; we hoped
he might help us find some solution to the problem. When
he got there, he could scarcely control his rage. No matter
what we said, his grim response was, "I am going to shoot
the man who is torturing that bear."

I had never seen him so upset. Our efforts to calm him
had no effect; I was beginning to think his threats might be
more than just sound and fury. Finally I convinced him to
wait until I had given it a try. He was skeptical, but he
agreed.

That afternoon, I went to the bazaar and found the bear's owner resting in the shade near the cage. I sat down by his side, and we exchanged a few polite words. He asked me where I came from. His eyes lit up when I told him I was from Kerala, where we are very fond of bears. "That's a nice one you've got there," I remarked. "Had him for very long?"

"Oh, he came as a young fellow."

"He seems a bit depressed," I said. "Do you suppose he needs some exercise?"

"Oh, yes," he said slowly. There was a note of apology in his voice, as if the question were already weighing heavily on him. Then he fell silent again, perhaps waiting for the inevitable reproach. When I too was silent, he went on. "I wish he had a bigger cage, but I can't afford it. I've got a family to support."

We talked for a while. When I took my leave, I went to see a carpenter who lived nearby. I told this man about the bear and about his owner's predicament, and he agreed to make a nice middle-class bear house – not just an adequate cage, but a comfortable home – for only a nominal fee. Then I went to see a lumber merchant. He seemed a little surprised to see a professorial type like me buying wood for a bear cage, but before long he was on the same bear wavelength. As I left, he said with a grin, "This is probably the only bear in India that will be living in a teak house."

Finally I went back to my friend, who was reasonably well to do, and said, "I have asked you for two days. Well, if you'll provide the financial resources, the bear will have a beautiful, spacious house by the end of the week."

My friend was quite surprised. "What happened?"

I told him the whole story. I don't think I have ever seen him happier. "How did you do all this?" he asked as he wrote out the check.

"I was as angry as you that the bear should be treated so cruelly, but I put my anger to work. With the power of my anger, I arranged for a new house for the bear and won over the owner – and I won you over, too."

"Touché," he said, laughing.

The carpenter was very skilled, and in his enthusiasm to help the bear, he worked overtime to make a beautiful little teak house, with lots of room to move about. When we took this bear-house to the bazaar, it was hard to tell who was more pleased – the man or his bear. They stayed for a few more days before moving on to another town, and I must confess that I went every day to the bazaar to watch that bear striding back and forth. To my loving eyes he seemed to be saying, "Thank you – how good of you to put your anger to work."

Anger is a tremendous power that can be used either to destroy life or to preserve and enhance it. I was just as angry as my friend. If I had not learned through meditation to conserve and harness my deeper resources, the anger that made the bear a new home could just as easily have led us all to grief.

Recently, I have had the privilege to use this skill again, but in a much larger context. A few years ago I saw a television documentary on the plight of African elephants, who are being killed at a rate of over one hundred thousand each year, and whose total population has been cut in half – from 1.3 million to just 625,000 – during the last decade. At present rates, if something is not done to protect them, they could be on the verge of extinction before the end of this century.

The scenes of suffering in that film haunted me all night. I felt terribly angry that such noble, gentle animals – as John Donne called them, "Nature's great masterpiece" – should

be driven toward extinction; and for no other reason than
to provide ivory jewelry and piano keys. But I did not let
this wave of anger overwhelm me. Instead, the next morning I plunged deep within myself in meditation, and with
the inspiration it brought me I sat down with my friends to
do something to help the elephants. On that same day we
formed a small organization, and when we came to naming
the group, our choice was easy. We call the group by the
same name as the gentle elephant on which I learned to ride,
which was so dear to my grandmother: Hasti.

Hasti is still a small group; yet it, and its younger coun-
terpart drawn from among my friends' children, Friends
of WildLife or FOWL, have already been instrumental in
saving many African elephants, by supporting the work
of researchers in the field and by influencing stores in this
country to stop selling ivory.

The children have been able to help directly, too. A few
years ago they got word, through a dedicated friend working in Africa, of a problem that had arisen in Kenya, near
Amboseli Park. A Masai village, located along an elephant
migratory route, was losing its crops to the hungry elephants. As a result, each year some thirty elephants were
killed as the villagers resorted to spears in a desperate attempt to save their food supply. Our friend proposed a
solar-powered electric fence to protect the crops. The Masai
welcomed the idea: they would gladly put up the fence, but
where would the money come from? The children threw
themselves heart and soul into fundraising. Before long,
the fence was installed, and both the elephants and the
crops were saved.

The wider ramifications of our elephant project reach far
into the future and touch on several of the pressing political
issues of our day. Perhaps most important, the elephant is a

vital link in the forest savannah ecosystem of Africa. Its loss would seriously jeopardize the ecological stability of these regions, with grave implications not only for animals but for the developing nations that depend on that forest for cooking fuel and for protection against desertification. By forging a link of compassion between people in the developed world and those in the Third World, we feel we are making a small but significant contribution to world peace, and helping to heal the wounds of Africa's colonial past.

This may seem like a small step on a very long journey; but, as I will narrate in the next section, small steps, when taken in the right spirit, and when we keep on taking them, can carry us a long, long way.

Infinite Resources

> Where there is despair, hope;
> Where there is darkness, light;
> Where there is sadness, joy.

Have you ever wondered what it would be like to be fabulously wealthy – to have so much that you could afford to give to any cause or charity you wanted, and change the world with your largesse? This is exactly the fruit of meditation. Meditation allows us to enter the unconscious consciously and unlock the tremendous resources hidden there, trapped in the conditioned habits of thought that have turned our most powerful inner assets into liabilities.

In these three lines, Saint Francis directs us to a tremendous source of energy that, because we have not learned to harness it, is limiting our enjoyment of life and crippling our efforts to make the earth a greener, healthier place: sorrow.

Many people get depressed by the current state of the

world. The sheer vastness of the problems we face is daunting, and it is only natural to feel terrible grief when we read about millions of acres of forests being burned, or several species becoming extinct every day, or the atmosphere being dangerously altered.

Yet few people realize what a valuable resource for change this grief is. Quite often, in fact, when I suggest trusteeship as a remedy for the environmental crises that face us, I am told that this is too small a solution, too tiny a drop in the ocean. "Me? What can a little person like me do?" people ask me again and again. "There's so little time left, and there are so many people who don't see the connections. So what if I stop using plastic cups and start planting a few trees? How much can that do?" I always appreciate questions like these – they often come from people who care deeply and whose despair arises from a desire to *solve* the problem rather than just get by until tomorrow. To be well adjusted in a wrong situation is a very dubious achievement.

I am not a theoretical person, and I never answer such questions theoretically. Instead, I usually narrate an incident from my own experience – an incident in which grief at the suffering of other creatures helped make a lasting, positive impact in several areas, affecting the way more than a million people treat the environment, each other, and other living creatures.

One day, as I was walking near our home on the Blue Mountain, I saw a man leading a little black calf to slaughter. To me, the calf's large, dark eyes seemed to be pleading, "Are you going to let this happen to me?" I was deeply upset – not only by my grief for the calf but by the realization that there were countless more like him. Then and there I decided that at every opportunity I would put in

a good word for animals. I did not know then where that
would lead me.

My ancestral family has been vegetarian for centuries,
so I grew up with a natural appreciation for the beauty of a
vegetarian way of life. When I first came to this country in
1959, I was sorry to see that vegetarian cooking, while not
altogether unheard of, was extremely rare. It was almost
impossible to find a vegetarian meal in any restaurant; to
tell the truth, I remember eating quite a bit of ice cream.
Before long, though, my friends and I got together and
began experimenting with California's abundant variety
of vegetables, grains, and fruits; a few of us even special-
ized in researching the nutritional requirements of a healthy
vegetarian diet. The eventual result was one of the first complete vegetarian cookbooks in the United States, *Laurel's
Kitchen*. It presents the beauty and healthy common sense
of vegetarian eating, and has sold over a million copies.

What we did not realize when we began, but what has
become abundantly clear in recent years, is that *Laurel's
Kitchen* is also a handbook for the preservation of rain forests and endangered species and for the reduction of the
greenhouse effect. Now – in 1989 – there are ten million
vegetarians in this country; each one of those ten million,
by reducing America's demand for imported beef, is saving
an acre of rain forest each year. Through the power of meditation, the sorrow I felt at seeing that beautiful calf's life cut
short was transformed into a fortune in active compassion,
which enabled my friends and me to play a part in saving
more than a million acres of rain forest annually: not because we are great people, but because that is the way the
compassionate universe works. You do not have to be rich
or famous or powerful to make a difference. When you
work in cooperation with others, motivated by compassion

and using thrifty, artistic means, your actions send ripples of positive change in every direction.

To be able to transform your anger or grief into a force for positive change is one of life's most exhilarating challenges. When I hear about young people surfing the twenty-five-foot waves at Waimea Bay, I often wish I could introduce them to this skill. That's the kind of daring and dedication it takes not to be swept away by anger or fear or greed, but to catch those towering waves that roll across the mind and ride them to a more peaceful, healthier planet.

I am prepared to make a bold claim for the way of life I am presenting here: the person who looks upon his or her entire life as a trust – body, talents, training, compassion, intelligence, and especially the heart's deepest fears, anger, and sorrows – such a person will never burn out, feel defeated, or get depressed or bored.

The Japanese have a little doll called the "daruma doll." If you push it down, it bounces right up again. That is how you can be: nothing will be able to keep you down, no matter how hard the blow, how fierce the storm. In fact, when you get good at it, you will look forward to storms, as Gandhi did, because every crisis will be an opportunity to reach deeper into the bottomless well of compassion and creativity within. You will actually be able to thrive on stress.

This is the challenge we face as we embark on the last decade of the twentieth century: to transform ourselves, each in our own small way, as Ashoka and Francis and Gandhi did; to rebel against the conditioning that keeps us bound in a self-destructive way of life; to take all the immense wealth of our hearts and place it in trust for the welfare of the world. There is no greater challenge than this, nor is there greater satisfaction.

George Bernard Shaw put it beautifully: "This is the true joy in life: the being used for a purpose recognized by yourself as a mighty one, the being thoroughly worn out before you're thrown on the scrap heap; the being a force of nature instead of a feverish little clod of ailments and grievances complaining that the world will not devote itself to making you happy."

When you jump up every morning eager to contribute to life and drop into bed every night deliciously tired because you have given your best without seeking anything in return, you will see love in the eyes of all around you, acknowledging the nobility of human nature they see in you. And even the most confirmed cynic, when he sees you forgiving and even befriending those who strike at you, will not be able to help saying – if only under his breath – "How I wish I could be like that."

Without Boundaries

*Molecules don't have passports. All the
creatures on Earth are in this together.
We need a primary allegiance to the
species and to planet Earth.*
      –Carl Sagan

*Love of one's country is a fine thing,
but why should love stop at the border?*
      –Pablo Casals

In November 1988, three California gray whales were found trapped off Point Barrow, Alaska. Separated from the ocean by a huge ridge of ice and shut off from the air by a thick surface ice pack, the whales had exhausted themselves butting the ice again and again with their heads. Without help, it was announced, they would suffocate.

That week in November, this small incident – of a sort that had gone practically unnoticed for years – brought forth an extraordinary response from people around the world. On television and in newspapers, millions of people watched as scientists, oil company personnel, Eskimos, and Soviet icebreakers teamed up to free the whales, cutting a series of breathing holes through the six-inch-thick ice pack and breaking through the ridge to clear a path to the open sea.

Quite a few commentators were surprised at the enthusiasm with which so many countries and individuals responded to the plight of a few whales, yet it made perfect sense to me. It is my experience that, in spite of all we hear to the contrary, our greatest need as human beings is to relieve suffering. Whose heart did not leap when one of the trapped whales lifted its head to the Eskimo who had pierced the ice for him? When we saw that image, we stopped bucking the current of unity that underlies life. For that moment we were one with the Eskimo and the whale, and it gave us joy.

Looking further, I would suggest an even deeper reason for the story's appeal: it holds hope for us. At first, those whales had been given up for dead; there was no hope for them, and perhaps they knew that themselves. We are like those whales – icebound by our environmental, social, and political problems. We too are sometimes given up for dead. Yet, despite all the monumental problems facing us, when we catch even a glimpse of the connections that link us with other living beings, we leap at the chance to relieve their suffering.

Small examples of compassion like these can teach us a great deal about where to begin in resolving much larger and more complex issues. Once compassion is aroused in our hearts, our potential to solve problems expands enormously. The boundaries that separate nation from nation, race from race, and individual from individual vanish, and possibilities arise that never existed before. Soviets, Americans, environmentalists, oilmen, Eskimos, and whalers all accomplished together what was impossible when they thought themselves at odds. Think of all we can do if we overcome our differences and work together like this for the tropical rain forests, or the African elephants, or the air our children will breathe.

This little incident stands out in sharp contrast to much of what we read and see today. In the media, in politics, in commerce, even in our personal lives, the emphasis is on the rigid boundaries between us. We live in a world defined not by similarities but by differences, not by connections but by separations.

Most obvious, of course, are the borders between nations. We draw a line around our own country and defend it with destructive weapons, hoping in this way to establish a secure and peaceful world for our children. Yet, as the world spends nearly a trillion dollars a year on armaments and the military, the effect is just the opposite. Not only does this waste of money, energy, and talent create a climate of intense suspicion and hostility that is itself a terrible threat to our children's safety, but it does nothing to defend us against the greatest threat to our children's future, the degradation of the environment.

However fiercely we try to defend our borders against armed invasion, no defense can protect us from the effects of another country's pollution. Smog produced in Detroit poisons lakes in Canada. Radioactive fallout from Chernobyl threatens children in the Netherlands. Toxic chemicals released into the Rhine river in Switzerland harm seals in the North Sea. During the nineteen-eighties we came to understand that pollution is a problem that transcends national boundaries. No single country can flourish unless all change their ways.

Many environmentalists and farsighted leaders are now acknowledging, however, that these are not just problems for experts or politicians to grapple with. The real solution must come from all of us as individuals. "The capacity of national leaders and of international institutions will be severely tested in the effort to put the world on a firm ecological and economic footing," the Worldwatch Institute states in its 1989 *State of the World* report. "Yet in the end, it is we as individuals who are being tested. Our values collectively shape social priorities – what policies are formulated, how resources are used, and when change begins to occur." The real environmental problems begin not at the frontiers between nations but at the boundaries that define and limit our own lives and minds.

All of us have the tendency, often without realizing it, to draw a line around what is ours. Within that area is all we care about: our success at work, our family's health, our car, our convenience, our prestige, our fun, our profit. Most of the time, we see only what is within that circle and no further. Outside it, unseen and uncared for, is the rest of life: other people, other creatures, the health of Mother Earth.

The conditioning of industrial civilization has encouraged this tendency in every possible way – and has discouraged our every attempt to outgrow it. It has convinced us we are all separate, competing consumers, that our happiness and security depend on our possessions and private satisfactions. The way of life based on this conditioning is what Gandhi refers to as pleasure without conscience, and its legacy is a world in which there seems to be an unresolvable conflict between our happiness and the happiness of others. Indeed, tragically, it has turned out to be a world in which our search for happiness is actually founded on the misery of other people and creatures, whether they be Amazon rubber tappers deprived of homes and livelihood as rain forest is cleared for cattle ranching, homeless people in our own cities who go hungry while we spend billions on missiles and bombs, elephants killed to make bracelets and billiard balls, or seals strangled by discarded six-pack yokes.

Sadly, we have not found lasting satisfaction either. Sociologists have their hands full trying to catalog the difficulties our society faces: broken relationships, drug violence in the streets and domestic violence in the home, a pervasive sense of loneliness and emptiness even among the most affluent, an earth in danger of becoming uninhabitable. Contrary to expectations, we are not becoming happier or more secure. Pleasure without conscience has also turned out to be pleasure without fulfillment or love – perhaps even without a future.

This is not because we are evil or cruel. Nor is it because "that's just the way human beings are." It is because we are trapped in a way of life that is suffocating everything noble and wise in us. The conditioning of profit and personal gratification is slowly closing us off from our greatest sources of joy: our compassion, our feeling of being needed, our kinship with the rest of life.

The purpose of meditation and the supporting practices of trusteeship is to break holes in this thick crust of conditioning that has kept us trapped, separated from the rest of life and unaware of our tremendous power to heal ourselves and the earth. To free ourselves completely is an extremely difficult task, yet even the smallest opening is enough to give us an intoxicating, inspiring glimpse of our real self.

It does not matter how small that opening is: your deepest self will be waiting eagerly on the other side. And if you persist, you will eventually find that you are surrounded by friends. They too, inspired by your example, will be chipping resolutely at the ice.

"Star to Every Wandering Bark"

In the second half of his prayer, Francis provides a short but comprehensive manual for erasing boundaries between nations and between individuals. The love these lines direct us to is the foundation of a trustee's life, and the source of his or her enormous power to change the way people treat each other and the earth.

> O Divine Master, grant that I may not so much seek
> To be consoled as to console,
> To be understood as to understand,
> To be loved as to love;
> For it is in giving that we receive;
> It is in pardoning that we are pardoned;
> It is in dying [to self] that we are born to eternal life.

In today's climate, Francis's idea of love is nothing short of revolutionary. Where Madison Avenue implies that love is something we fall into as we would a manhole, Francis speaks of it as a grand staircase, stretching upward from our feet to the highest summit of human experience, from which we can look down and see all people, all creatures, and all life as one and indivisible.

For Francis, love bears no resemblance to a business venture; it has nothing to do with accounts receivable or payable. In this too, he contradicts current theories. It's not unusual these days to see magazines recommending that couples draw up contracts listing what each partner expects from the other: he will take her out on the town at least once a week; she will cook him a candlelight dinner at least twice a week.

When I see those articles, I can't help thinking of Shakespeare's King Lear. "Which of you shall we say doth love us most?" he asks his daughters as he prepares to divide his kingdom among them. One by one the three daughters respond, and their answers reveal the quality of their love.

Attracted by the prospect of a rich dowry, Regan and Goneril each play up to the old king. Lear is pleased by their lavish praise and rewards each of them with a portion of the kingdom.

Then comes young Cordelia's turn. Unlike the others, she loves her father without wanting anything in return, and she has been listening with embarrassment to her sisters. "My love's more richer than my tongue," she whispers to herself, wondering how she could ever match their exaggerations. When Lear turns to her, expecting the most honeyed compliments from his favorite daughter, she simply tells him the truth: that she loves and honors him as a daughter should.

This is a profound study in love. Cordelia's love has nothing to do with business; she simply offers her father the unchanging love and respect she has shown him all along – not in pretty words she cannot find, but in her daily actions, regardless of what he gives or does not give her. In one of his later sonnets, Shakespeare wrote eloquently of the kind of love I imagine Cordelia felt for Lear – the kind of love that transcends all obstacles and all boundaries. There are few descriptions of love to match it in the literature of any time or country I know of:

> Love is not love
> Which alters when it alteration finds,

Or bends with the remover to remove:
O, no! it is an ever-fixèd mark,
That looks on tempests and is never shaken;
It is the star to every wandering bark,
Whose worth's unknown, although his height be taken.
Love's not Time's fool, though rosy lips and cheeks
Within his bending sickle's compass come;
Love alters not with his brief hours and weeks,
But bears it out even to the edge of doom.

Tragically, the king cannot recognize Cordelia's love. He places his faith in the flatterers, who are only seeking their own ends. Betrayed by them, he ends up wandering the moors alone except for his court fool, having lost not only his kingdom but his beloved Cordelia as well.

When it comes to love, we too are at the bottom of the staircase, unaware that there is anything above us. Like Lear, we are taught to ask the question, "How much do you love me?" Rarely, if ever, do we ask "How much do I love you?" or "How can I love you more?" Those magazine articles are passé. We are already conditioned to treat love as a kind of contract, saying to our family or partner or friend, "If you give me this much love, I'll give that much back. If I give you a little more, you must pay it back or I'll find someone else who will." This has gone to such extremes that many people find it difficult to develop a lasting relationship. Through no fault of their own, they have known the loneliness and pain that drove Lear to cry as he stood on the moors: "You see me here, you gods, a poor old man, as full of grief as age. . . ."

The Path To Freedom

In chapter 6, I presented the first half of Francis's prayer as a way for any individual to learn to transform powerful emotions like anger or despair into constructive, compassionate action. In this chapter, I shall interpret the second half of the prayer as a manual for daily living: a guide for anyone who wants to live free from conditioning, treating body, resources, and talents as a valuable trust for the welfare of the world. To me, these lines form a kind of condensed textbook for learning how to love.

The program of trusteeship and meditation I am discussing here is designed to help you teach yourself this essential skill. I take no credit for inventing it. I have simply adapted to modern life several methods of mental training that can be found in every major spiritual tradition. They contain nothing I have not tested in my own life and found to be successful – not in an isolated hermitage but in the midst of an active career, teaching, lecturing, and writing. It is my hope that they can serve as a modern equivalent of what the psychologist William James called the highest kind of education: the conscious remaking of one's own life and character through the training of the mind.

As I mentioned earlier, I always recommend that meditation be accompanied by a series of supporting practices, to ensure that the increased concentration and energy which meditation brings will be translated into beneficial changes in our way of living. Here I will take a look at four of those supporting practices as they pertain to Francis's great insights into the nature of love.

1. Developing One-Pointed Attention.

"May I not so much seek to be consoled as to console," Francis begins, "to be understood as to understand, to be loved as to love."

Love begins, Francis is saying, not when long-stem roses and a box of chocolate truffles arrive on your doorstep, but when you learn to forget yourself. Currently, popular opinion seems to hold that if we forget our private interests, we are likely to develop some neurosis or turn into zombies. It is rarely understood that some of the most accomplished men and women of our times have achieved greatness through this very skill of forgetting themselves.

If you talk to athletes or artists or scientists, most will tell you they are happiest when they are working hard, with all their faculties fully engaged in a challenging project. In fact, the most successful ones are those who can lose themselves completely in their work. Over two thousand years ago, the Indian philosopher Patanjali examined such mental dynamics with the kind of meticulous precision we have come to associate with modern science. His conclusion sheds light not only on sports and art and science, but on all of life: when the scientist is completely concentrated on his research, when the athlete has no other thought than her game, Patanjali would say, they have forgotten themselves – and that is why they are happy.

The ability to forget oneself is the key to happiness and success in any field. When great painters or dancers or musicians are completely focused on their art, they are not happy because of the painting or the music or the dance. They are happy because they have left behind the petty irritations and frustrations that go with self-interest: trying to decide what you want, how you will get it, whom you will have to compete with for it, what you will do with it when you have it, what you will want after you have become tired of it, and so on.

When we concentrate deeply, even for just a few moments, there is a respite from this ceaseless conflict between conditioned self-interest and our desire to love; there is a short truce in the war between pleasure and conscience. The trouble is that most people – even great scientists and artists – have, at best, only partial control over their attention. Even when they can forget themselves at work, the battle rages on during the rest of the day and night. We rarely realize it, but this conflict between pleasure and conscience, which is present in everyone's mind, is a constant drain on our energy and vital capacities.

It is as if two voices were speaking in our minds at once, competing for our attention. One voice, that of conditioning, is saying, "Look out for number one. Life's too short not to have and do everything you want. It is in grabbing that we receive." The other voice – love – speaks quietly from the innermost depths of our being, saying to the world, "Your cares are also my cares, and so are your joys. How can I be happy if you are miserable?" Like St. Francis in his "Canticle of the Sun," Love says not "Earth, the resource to be mined," but "Mother Earth, who sustains and governs us and brings forth varied fruits, bright flowers, and plants": not "Ocean, the receptacle for waste," but "Sister water, who is useful and humble, precious and pure."

Together with meditation, the practice of one-pointed attention – doing just one thing at a time, and giving it your full attention – can help you improve your ability to listen only to the voice of love. As you acquire this skill, you will begin to see that there is no real conflict between you and the rest of the world. What brings joy to your family, friends, and neighbors also brings joy to you, no matter how it affects your bank account or the amount of fun you have. You will find that the deeper your concentration becomes, the more artistically and creatively you will be able to work, the more richly you will enjoy the beauties of nature, and the more deeply you will be able to love. Each time you forget yourself in this way, you will get a glimpse of how it is to live without boundaries, in a world that is not divided by opinion or resentment. This is a first taste of real freedom.

2. *Repeating a Mantram*

Over the years, I have seen hundreds of romances spring up between young Romeos and Juliets in my classes. First they start sitting beside each other in class. A week or two later, they walk in holding hands. Another week and they are wearing his-and-hers jogging suits. But all too soon, I would see Romeo staring angrily out the window on one side of the room while Juliet distractedly files her nails on the other. In addition to my duties as professor, I often served as a kind of Dear Abby for my students, so after a time Romeo or Juliet would come to me and ask what went wrong. "Isn't she the right girl for me?" "Is he incapable of love? Am I?"

My answer usually surprised them. "None of the above," I would say. "There is nothing wrong with either of you. You're just not yet tough enough to be really in love."

According to Francis, the real basis for a loving relationship that grows instead of wanes is increasing tenderness, understanding, and respect for each other. In other words, if your girlfriend is rude to you, that is the time not to move away from her but to get closer. If your boyfriend is insensitive, that is when you need to be even more understanding. When she provokes you, become more loving. When he hinders you, become more tender.

Of course, this requires a great deal of inward toughness. When someone we love offends us or lets us down, it is only natural to want to retaliate. In the long run, no amount of "say it with flowers" or dancing cheek to cheek can substitute for the kind of toughness that enables us to remain loving and not to be swept away by that wave of anger. "Be tough and then say it with flowers," I used to tell my students. "Be understanding and then dance cheek to cheek."

It is terribly difficult to resist that wave of ill will when it rises, yet it can be done, and one of the most powerful aids in that process is a practice Gandhi recommended at every opportunity: the repetition of the mantram, or, as it is called in some traditions, the Holy Name.

A mantram is a powerful spiritual phrase that can be repeated silently at almost any time of the day. Following in Gandhi's footsteps, I suggest it not as a theory, but as a practical experiment that can be undertaken and verified by anyone.

Every religious tradition has a mantram, often more than one. For Christians, the name of Jesus itself is a powerful mantram. Catholics also use Hail Mary or Ave Maria. Jews may use *Barukh attah Adonai*, "Blessed art Thou, O Lord," or the Hasidic formula *Ribono shel olam*, "Lord of the universe." Muslims repeat the name of Allah or *Allahu akbar*, "God is great." Probably the oldest Buddhist mantram, and one that can be used by anyone who does not feel comfortable with the concept of a personal God, is *Om mani padme hum*, a beautiful phrase referring to the jewel of compassion in the lotus of the heart. From the many mantrams found in Hinduism, I recommend *Rama*, which was Mahatma Gandhi's mantram, or the longer version I received from my own spiritual teacher, my grandmother:

> *Haré Rama Haré Rama*
> *Rama Rama Haré Haré*
> *Haré Krishna Haré Krishna*
> *Krishna Krishna Haré Haré*

To begin, select a mantram that appeals to you deeply. Then repeat it silently whenever you get the chance: while walking, while waiting in line, while doing mechanical chores like washing dishes, and especially while you are falling asleep. You will find that this is not mindless repetition; the mantram will help to keep you relaxed and composed. Whenever you are angry or afraid, nervous or worried or resentful, repeat the mantram until the agitation subsides. The mantram works to steady the mind. All these emotions are power running against you, which the mantram can harness and put to work.

In fact, one of the most important uses of the mantram is in times of emotional agitation. When your boyfriend stands you up, or your girlfriend pokes fun at your athletic prowess, don't explode; instead, repeat your mantram silently in your mind, with all the energy that would have gone into anger. If possible, go for a really fast walk around the block at the same time. Before long, you will find that the rhythm of the mantram combines with the rhythm of your footsteps to change the rhythm of your breathing, which is closely connected with the rhythm of thinking.

In this way, the mantram enables you to slow down the thinking process. Like a highway patrol car slowing down traffic, the mantram weaves in and out between thoughts, separating them wider and wider until finally they are so far apart that you can choose what to think next. Where you used to say, "Get lost, get lost, get lost," you begin to say "Get . . . lost." A little later on, "G e t . . . l o s t." Finally, all your mind can muster is "G e t . . . ." Then, if you have been repeating the mantram whenever possible, you can start to replace "Get lost" with "How can I help that person?"

When I made this suggestion to my students at Berkeley, I used to get quite a few vociferous questions. "You mean I should be nice to that guy, after what he said about me?"

"That's it exactly."

"Ridiculous!"

"Ridiculous indeed," I answered, "but most beneficial – not just for him, but for you." Being kind is even good health insurance. Extensive medical studies suggest that chronic anger and hostility are associated with a greater risk of heart disease. Conversely, those who forgive easily, whose state of mind is naturally friendly, can cope more healthily with the normal stress of life.

Even more important than health, however, is the effect a kind response has on personal relationships. You will find that freeing yourself from instinctive, reflex reactions to difficult situations will enrich all your relationships – even with those who oppose you. When you are kind to a foe, he ceases to be a foe. In time, he may even turn out to be a friend.

Gandhi's life was filled with such relationships. Once, during Gandhi's campaigns for the rights of Indians in South Africa, he came before the head of the Transvaal government, General Jan Smuts. Gandhi had already developed the essentials of his later style, and it is easy to picture him sitting before this able Boer soldier and informing him quietly: "I want you to know I intend to fight against your government."

Smuts must have thought he was hearing things. "You have come here to tell me that?" he laughs. "Is there anything more you want to say?"

"Yes," says Gandhi. "I am going to win."

Smuts is astonished. "Well," he says at last, "and how are you going to do this?"

And Gandhi smiles. "With your help."

Years later Smuts admitted, not without humor, that this is exactly what Gandhi did. By his courage, and by the inward toughness that allowed him to stick it out without yielding and without retaliation, Gandhi managed at last to win the general's respect and friendship. Indeed, in 1939, on the occasion of Gandhi's seventieth birthday, Smuts returned a pair of sandals Gandhi had made while imprisoned in South Africa and given to Smuts in 1914. "I have worn these sandals for many a summer since then," Smuts said, "even though I may feel that I am not worthy to stand in the shoes of so great a man."

When people accorded Gandhi such high praise, he never accepted it for himself. Instead, he often gave the credit to his mantram, on which he relied for faith and courage in the severe trials he faced almost every day.

3. *Training the Senses*

Let me make it very clear: living like this does not mean diluting your principles or becoming a doormat for more aggressive people. On nonessentials, compromising gracefully helps to oil the wheels of life; but when people oppose you on something of central importance, I am not in favor of taking one step backwards. By using the mantram you can learn to stand firm just where you are, listening with respect and maintaining your position with goodwill yet never retaliating or retreating. To be able to disagree without being disagreeable is a valuable art.

In fact, one of the surest signs of love is the capacity to say no tenderly but firmly when someone is about to harm himself or others. Children in particular cannot help being educated when parents can say no without withdrawing their love and support. Unfortunately, many parents find it difficult to oppose their children at all. I would agree with the psychologists who say this is not love but a lack of love. They are not really thinking about their child, but about themselves.

This applies in the larger context as well. When we do

nothing to halt the devastation of our environment, we are betraying a serious lack of love, not only for our own children but for children everywhere. We all have the option to act as trustees, showing through quiet, persuasive personal example how to say no to the many aspects of modern civilization that harm the environment without benefiting anyone. By becoming vegetarian, for example, we can say, "No, cutting down rainforests to raise beef endangers everybody's air." Carpools are a way of saying, "No, it profits no one to ruin the air and waste our fossil fuels." By not buying and using unnecessary plastic products, we say, "No, we don't need these things, we don't need the additional pollution, and we don't need any more garbage."

In order to say no gracefully and without acrimony, however, your convictions must run deep, and this does not happen overnight. Little by little, meditation and these supporting practices carry your ideals deep into your personality, where their light will shine through every aspect of your life.

One excellent method for deepening your convictions is to begin gradually to make some of the changes I suggested in chapter five: in the food you eat, the things you buy, the way you use your car. In all of these, conditioning has made us subject to the dictatorship of rigid likes and dislikes. To free ourselves from this conditioning, we need to be able to change our likes and dislikes freely when it is in the best interests of those around us or our environment.

Like any physical training program, this process – which I call training the senses – requires constant effort and sustained enthusiasm. Making changes in long-held habits is a bit like dislodging an old, firmly rooted tree stump: you pull and pull, and nothing seems to happen. But I have had the privilege of helping many people get rid of unwanted habits and addictions by teaching them how to use meditation and the supporting practices as a pick and shovel for digging deep into consciousness until they can loosen the habit's roots and pull it out like a weed.

The purpose of training the senses is not simply to help the environment, but to build such will and quiet confidence that you cannot be overrun by Madison Avenue or any other sort of conditioning. When necessary, you will have the freedom to say no – not with anger or resentment, but with artistry and gentle humor. Nothing can so disarm an opponent or defuse a tense situation, whether between individuals or between nations.

Considering the enormous challenges we will face in coming decades, it would be helpful to cultivate an artful blend of gentle humor and unbreakable resolution. I enjoyed, for instance, Carl Sagan's pungent reply to a bureaucrat's suggestion that to remedy the depletion of the ozone layer, we need do nothing more than wear sunglasses and hats. Sagan explained that the increase in ultraviolet radiation would affect adversely all kinds of life, including bacteria that are essential to the rice crop on which billions of people depend. "Shall we provide a hat and sunglasses to every bacterium?" he asked. Let us try in all our work to communicate our differences like this, with pain in heart and tongue in cheek.

4. *Putting Others First*

Our age has been called the age of anger, and it is true that we are living in one of the most violent periods in history. But there is no reason for anybody to be left to the mercy of these storms, whether they be physical or verbal, whether they happen on the streets, on the battlefield, or in the home. Meditation and the allied disciplines enable you to take your convictions deeper and deeper into consciousness, so that they become a constant source of strength and security – even when you are severely challenged or threatened.

Whatever your field of activity, this is a most valuable asset. Life does not always throw roses; sometimes it throws tomatoes, or even hefty bricks. Today someone praises you, tomorrow they will blame you. Today your friends appreciate you, tomorrow the same friends will deprecate you – that is the nature of the world. But if your convictions and your desire to love are established deep in your consciousness, your conduct will not be influenced by anger or the desire to retaliate. At the depths, you will be unaffected when others are hostile to you, so you will be free to respond in a way that helps both them and yourself. It is not that you will not suffer or be hurt, but you will no longer get afraid and try to run away. You will feel the grief of others deeply, but you will also have the resources to help them.

The more you look upon your life as a trust for the benefit of others, the less complicated – and the more effective and satisfying – your work and relationships will become. For most of us, dealing with other people is a very laborious process. "If I do this, is he going to like me?" "If I don't do this, how is she going to react?" Dwelling on ourselves like this exhausts us and undermines our security. Those who keep on thinking about *their* own needs, *their* wants, *their* plans, *their* ideas cannot help becoming lonely and insecure. The simple but effective technique I recommend is to learn to put other people first – beginning within the circle of your family and friends, where there is already a basis of love to build on. When husband and wife try to put each other first, for example, they are not only moving closer to each other; they are also removing the boundaries that separate them from the rest of life, which deepens their relationships with everyone else as well.

By putting the welfare of those around you first, you will gradually find it natural to focus your energy and creativity into a single sharp beam: how much can I give to those around me? Instead of asking "How much will I get?" or "What will they think of me?" your only question will be, "How much can I contribute to this situation?" The trustee's motto is "I give, therefore I am."

Sometimes I picture the mind as a freeway with many wide lanes leading to loneliness and despair – lanes like anger, greed, and fear. On the other side of the freeway, there is just one narrow lane that heads toward peace and a healthy earth: the lane of love. When you meditate on the prayer of St. Francis, going through the verses as slowly as possible, bringing your attention back every time it wanders – even if you have to bring it back twenty times in the space of a half hour – you are learning to drive your mind in one and the same lane: the lane of love, patience, and forgiveness. And during the day, by trying not to dwell on your personal interests but focusing instead on the needs of others, you can deepen the effectiveness of your meditation.

Once you have learned this marvelous skill of staying in the same lane, always putting the welfare of others first, you become free to respond with skill and judgment, even under fierce attack. In order to get angry or greedy or afraid, the mind has to change lanes. When you have learned to drive in only one lane, no attack or misfortune can make you unloving or unwise.

When you love like this, you begin to know what real freedom is. Nothing can keep you from loving. You live in a world that is whole, no longer divided between allies and enemies, exploiter and exploited. You swim free in a sea of love, at home with all people, all nature, and all creatures.

If I could rewrite Shakespeare's play, I would cast King Lear as a person who learns from Cordelia never to ask "How much do you love me?" Instead he would resolve to love more: Goneril, Regan, Cordelia, even the Fool. Goneril would accomplish far less evil, for she would not be able to draw power by playing on his affections; Cordelia would not have to die to try to save him. In the evening of his life he would turn his face to the stars and say, "Look upon a man as full of joy as he is of love."

Martin Luther King, Jr. was one of many who have learned from Gandhi the tremendous power of such love. "I had almost despaired of the power of love in solving social problems," wrote Dr. King in 1960. "The 'turn the other cheek' philosophy and the 'love your enemies' philosophy are only valid, I felt, when individuals are in conflict with other individuals. . . . As I delved deeper into the philosophy of Gandhi my skepticism concerning the power of love gradually diminished. . . ." He explained, "Gandhi was probably the first person in history to lift the love ethic of Jesus above mere interaction between individuals to a powerful and effective social force on a large scale."

In the following excerpt from a talk Dr. King gave in 1967, listen to the freedom that kind of unconditional love gave him – a freedom that transformed even virulent enemies into brothers and sisters, and that no outside force, however cruel or violent, could crush:

> I've seen too much hate to want to hate. . . . Somehow we must be able to stand up before our most bitter opponents and say: "We shall match your capacity to inflict suffering by our capacity to endure suffering. We will meet your physical force with soul force. Do to us what you will

and we will still love you. We cannot in all good conscience obey your unjust laws and abide by the unjust system, because noncooperation with evil is as much a moral obligation as is cooperation with good, and so throw us in jail and we will still love you. Bomb our homes and threaten our children, and, as difficult as it is, we will still love you. Send your hooded perpetrators of violence into our communities at the midnight hour and drag us out on some wayside road and leave us half-dead as you beat us, and we will still love you. Send your propaganda agents around the country, and make it appear that we are not fit, culturally and otherwise, for integration, and we'll still love you. But be assured that we'll wear you down by our capacity to suffer, and one day we will win our freedom. We will not only win freedom for ourselves; we will so appeal to your heart and conscience that we will win you in the process, and our victory will be a double victory.

Through the practice of meditation and the supporting practices, every one of us can learn to love like this. In all our relationships – with our parents, our partner, our children, our friends, even our enemies – we can humbly but irresistibly blaze a trail for the world to follow. With every detail of our lives we can make a statement: In the battle to save the earth, the people of the world are all on the same side; on the other side are war, violence, greed, self-interest, and fear.

We need that inspiration more than ever. "If, as it sometimes seems, nations require an adversary to maintain their cohesiveness," writes James R. Udall, "let global warming be the foil – it's the common enemy. Though ancient antagonisms won't vanish overnight, armies are vestigial from an ecological perspective: The globe needs tree-planters more than soldiers." Let us take up these ancient tools for training the mind, which are the equal property of all the great spiritual traditions, and free ourselves from the confinement of those "ancient antagonisms" – the centuries of enmity separating country from country, race from race, individual from individual.

Erasing the Boundaries

As I grew more and more dedicated to the practice of meditation, I found the boundaries by which I had separated myself from others slowly disappearing. It surprised me to realize that I was beginning to feel always at home, no matter where I was or with whom. I noticed this especially on my first trip to the United States. I was traveling by steamship, stopping at ports of call to visit some of the great cities of the Middle East and Europe, and I remember sitting one beautiful afternoon on a park bench in Paris, watching school children at play. Later, when I dined with a friend, he asked me how I found the Parisians. I answered, "They're no different from Indians." Seated there in a place I had never seen, surrounded by a language I did not know, I felt completely at home.

Well, perhaps everyone feels at home in Paris. But in my case, that comment signified a momentous change taking place at the deepest level of my consciousness. Where I used to identify people on the basis of how they differed from me in language, politics, or personality, now those differences seemed superficial. I had begun to perceive – not just to think, but to know with every fiber of my being – that our differences are only one percent of who we are. The other ninety-nine percent is common to all living creatures. All creatures love life, said the Buddha, and all creatures fear death. These are common truths that transcend every particular of skin and behavior and opinion.

In ordinary consciousness, our conditioned self-interest limits us to seeing and paying attention only to that one percent of difference – to the almost total exclusion of our common humanity. Occasionally we do catch a glimpse of how much we all have in common, as when we behold great beauty, or when we are united by a powerful desire for peace or justice. But such moments come rarely, and are swallowed up all too quickly by a flood of conditioned thinking that once again rivets our attention on how this person insulted us or that country offended us, how life would be perfect if only we had just a bit more money or our opinions were shared by those in power.

It is a fine thing to be able to see and enjoy the little differences between people – the color of their skin, the language they speak, the name of their God. Those details are a precious and expressive part of who we are. But they are only a tiny part. Such a minuscule fraction is nothing to build a life on, or a political theory or economic policy.

When I experienced this change in perspective, it was as if all the boundary lines had been erased between myself and other people, between my country and other countries, between myself and the rest of life. Human beings of all races, even animals, birds, fish, all had become like family to me; I could no longer say where their happiness left off and mine began. By the alchemy of self-transformation – which would have been beyond my reach without the tremendous inspiration and guidance of my grandmother – my vision had cleared and I could see that those Parisian children, and all the other children of the world, were not just children: they were *my* children, as dear to me as life itself.

All of us have moments when we sense how much we have in common with the rest of life. The recognition may come in a small way, as when we see a whale struggling for its life and suddenly realize how dear life is to it; or it may come at times of historic importance, as when we listen to a leader like Mahatma Gandhi or Martin Luther King, Jr.

Something makes us realize that the life we know and love is not different from the life others know and love, and that the powerful current flowing through us also flows through the hearts of those around us.

Glimpses of this truth are enshrined in our works of art, our literature, our religion, our philosophy. When we hear Yevgeny Yevtushenko saying, "Every bullet is aimed at the heart of a mother," we can feel national boundaries vanish. When we are deeply moved by a piece of music or a play or a dance, a tiny window opens onto the vast sea of our common experience, the unity of all life. For a moment we are not alone but together, humbled by beauty and the truth.

Yet even for the great artist these are only isolated moments, islands of peace in a world that knows far more about separateness than unity. It is all the more heartbreaking when we know that in a moment the boundaries will be redrawn, the window will slam shut, and the world will go back to hating and killing. It *is* heartbreaking, until we realize that it is unnecessary – utterly unnecessary.

When I realized this – when I saw that the boundaries could be erased forever from my heart never to be redrawn, that I need never return to the insignificance of a life based on separateness – I knew I had discovered the key to living in a compassionate universe. Because all of life is a seamless whole, our only real suffering comes when we try to separate ourselves from it, imagining that a line can be drawn to divide your sadness from my happiness, your poverty from my wealth, your country's war from my nation's peace, nature's destruction from my health. Every moment of every day we have the opportunity to erase a boundary – with a smile or kind word, with the details of an artistic, simple life, with a loving thought for Mother Earth.

The moment a human being erases these boundaries and ceases to live as a separate fragment concerned only with petty, individual interests, he or she releases an irresistible force for health and harmony into the world. Even a small group of such people, living a simple, self-reliant, loving life, will be enough to bring about far-reaching changes in our society.

Lighting the Lamp

> *I am utterly convinced that most of the great environmental struggles will be either won or lost in the 1990s. And that by the next century it will be too late.*
>
> —Thomas Lovejoy

> *There comes a time when an individual becomes irresistible and his action becomes all-pervasive in its effect. This comes when he reduces himself to zero.*
>
> —Mahatma Gandhi

On a bitterly cold winter night in 1893, at the small railway town of Maritzburg, South Africa, a young man was thrown off a train solely because of the color of his skin. Alone in a foreign country, he had come to South Africa as a last resort, hoping to establish a career that had eluded him in his native India.

"It was winter," he recalled later, "and winter in the higher regions of South Africa is severely cold. Maritzburg being at a high altitude, the cold was extremely bitter. My overcoat was in my luggage but I did not dare to ask for it lest I should be insulted again, so I sat and shivered. There was no light in the room."

Many years later, when Gandhi was asked by an American missionary what the most creative moment in his life had been, he said it was that night he spent in the railway station at Maritzburg, asking himself, "Shall I submit to this injustice? Or, for the sake of the thousands of people who are in the same situation, shall I work to change it?" The man who in thirty years' time would be called "Mahatma" made his choice.

That night, the flame of self-sacrifice leapt up in the heart of this ordinary young man. Every day afterwards, for the twenty years he spent in South Africa, he protected that flame. He relit it when it was blown out by strong winds. He fueled it with his every ounce of energy and desire and courage. By the time he returned to India, what had been a spark had grown into a bonfire that could never be extinguished, lighting and warming the whole world. The creation of a thousand forests is to be found in a single acorn, Ralph Waldo Emerson once wrote, and the flame of hope that Gandhi was to light in so many millions of hearts first flashed as a tiny spark in that remote railway station.

Almost a hundred years later, you and I and every other human being every day face a question no less difficult or inescapable than the one Gandhi wrestled with: "Shall I put aside my self-interest and work to remake my life, for the sake of the earth and the children who will inherit it?"

Tonight is our night at Maritzburg. How will we answer that question? Tomorrow morning, when we look in the mirror, what will we see – an insignificant acorn or the seed of a thousand forests?

Worship Without Self-Sacrifice

In his final diagnosis, worship without self-sacrifice, Gandhi drops a brilliant flare on the modern world. Worship and self-sacrifice: to grasp just how much one individual can heal the world, it is necessary to understand what Gandhi and the mystics really mean when they use those much-misrepresented words.

Someone once complained to G. K. Chesterton that the main problem with modern civilization is that people don't believe in anything anymore. "I disagree," Chesterton replied. "The real problem is that they will believe in anything at all." The worship Gandhi is talking about is not religious ceremonies; it is the worship we carry on every day in our hearts and minds. In the industrial era, we have not ceased to worship; we have only divided our capacity for devotion into a million and one fruitless, self-centered channels. We build shopping malls as if they were temples. I visited one mall recently that was paved in marble like Saint Peter's. People spend a great deal of their time and resources at such places, wandering from one store to another, gazing with longing at objects they hope will make them happy and fulfilled.

The brilliant psychologists of India's ancient spiritual tradition were among the first to recognize that every one of our desires is actually a prayer – a prayer that *will* be answered, though rarely in just the way we had anticipated. When a smoker reaches for a cigarette, they would say, he is praying to the god of nicotine to grant him pleasure, or at least a temporary respite from his craving. Tragically, doctors tell us he is also praying for emphysema and lung cancer. When we pray to the god of petroleum to help us save a little bit of time or to increase our profit margin, we are also praying for seas black with oil, a sky brown with smog, and a topsoil that blows away in the wind. A trustee recognizes the tremendous power of these unconscious prayers and, through meditation, learns to use that power to heal instead of to harm the earth.

After meticulous observation, those early Indian scientists of the mind laid out the mechanics of desire in a formula that is, to me, the spiritual equivalent of Einstein's $E = mc^2$:

> You are what your deep, driving desire is.
> As your deep, driving desire is, so is your will.
> As your will is, so is your deed.
> As your deed is, so is your destiny.

Like Einstein's formula, this epic statement points the way to a source of energy far exceeding our ordinary limitations. Today that energy is mostly wasted on unbeneficial pursuits, but with the training of the mind it can be harnessed to remake the human personality.

The goal of meditation is to get hold of our desires and draw them together into a single, all-consuming passion for the well-being of all of life. It is just like weaving many separate threads into a single, concentrated wick. The more closely you gather the threads, the more brightly your life will shine, illuminating not only your own home and family, but the lives of your friends, community, nation, and world.

In any field of endeavor, it is this unification of desires that brings concentration, perseverance, and success. The vast majority of people have many, many desires. Without the benefit of meditation, this often leads to one of the saddest of lives – a superficial one. Seeking little things, content with tiny successes centered around their personal appearance and possessions and pastimes, these are, to me, the poorest of people. They inhabit the "third world" of shallow consciousness.

But it is possible, through meditation and the supporting practices, to weave those many stray desires into just a few very powerful desires. The fewer your desires, the stronger each will be. People who have just a few strong desires usually make their mark in life whatever field they throw themselves into, because their available energy and concentration are enormous. Out of this camp come great poets, statesmen, musicians, and humanitarians.

But for those to whom fame and fortune are no substitute for a healthy, peaceful world, who cannot rest until they know for certain who they are and why they are alive, there is another, even loftier goal. Through meditation, it is possible for any one of us to join the company of those rare men and women whose lives are shaped by only one deep, driving desire: to grow to their full height as human beings. To use Tennyson's words, these are the true "movers and shakers" of the world.

In the language of orthodox religion, such people are men and women of God. In the language of a post-industrial era, it might be more fitting to use the term with which Gandhi described himself: these people aspire to be trustees of themselves and the earth. Their search is for the single spirit, present in all of us, to which the priceless resources of life truly belong.

The Coconut Tree

When I took up the practice of meditation, I was fortunate in having already developed a certain one-pointedness in my desires. Most of my energy and attention went into my teaching and literary activities. But as my meditation deepened, I gradually developed the desire to turn every aspect of my life into an instrument of service. I began to remember something my Granny had often told me: "In your life, try to be like the coconut tree."

Indeed, the coconut tree is a perfect symbol for the aspirations of a trustee. Every part of the tree is useful and beneficial. Coconut palms grow tall all over my native state of Kerala, and in the years of my childhood they provided us with everything from shelter to food: the branches were used for building roofs, the trunk for pillars, the roots for medicines, the water inside for drinking, the oil for cooking, the fruit for eating, the shell to make ladles and bowls, and the fiber for rope.

So, when I began to look upon my own life as a trust, I found that my passion for literature and teaching could become a very useful tool for serving life – as long as I did not use it for my own personal advancement but for sharing spiritual understanding with others. Curiously, it was when I stopped looking for a personal reward in teaching that I enjoyed it most, and taught better as well.

Everyone has some special passion or talent – often several – which can be enhanced and transformed through the practice of meditation. Scientists, gardeners, journalists, carpenters, teachers, cooks, mothers, fathers: we can all learn to harness the desires that have led us to our specialties, and turn those talents into a source of healing for those around us.

And, as I suggested before, meditation gradually gives us the ability to harness the selfish urges and impulses hiding in the subterranean depths of our hearts. If you feel greedy, you can learn to be greedy not just for yourself but for everyone, wanting all to be happy. If you feel the lust to possess or control another person, you can turn that lust into the desire to understand, help, and support those around you – a kind of lust for their needs instead of what you imagine to be your own. By training your mind to be detached from self-interest, you can turn sorrow and self-pity into a protective umbrella of compassion for all of life. And you can use the tremendous power locked up in anger to oppose corruption and injustice – not by destroying others, but by winning them over in love.

It is this transformation of desire that Gandhi is referring to when he speaks of self-sacrifice, and the life it leads to is just the opposite of dreary mortification. A trustee's life is a joyous, invigorating climb up the staircase of love, each step bringing new friendships and unearthing new talents, improving life not only for himself or herself, but for everyone around.

All you lose in taking up this challenge is your separateness, your loneliness, your fear, and your inability to change the way you live. And what do you gain? The electricity of harnessed desire magnifies your every capacity to serve and heal. Your life becomes a multiplication of joys and loves. If it is delightful to fall in love with one person, just imagine what it is like to fall in love with everyone. Imagine the joy of St. Francis, who fell in love not only with all people but with the animals and birds and streams and forests that surrounded him. As the Upanishads say, the joy of such a person is a million times greater than the happiness of even the most successful self-centered person.

There is a wonderful Indian story about a little boy

whose parents take him to a reception at the maharaja's
palace. A servant is circulating among the guests with a tray
of delicacies, and the boy is deeply impressed by the selec-
tion. When his turn comes, the servant sees the look in his
eyes and tells him firmly, "Choose just one item, please."

"Just one?"

"That's right."

"As long as it's just one thing, you'll give it to me?"

The servant, who has many more guests to attend to, is
getting a little impatient. "That's right," he says. "I'll give
you one item and one item only. What will it be?"

"The whole tray."

The maharaja, pleased by this daring, takes the heavily-
laden tray from the servant and himself presents it to the
boy.

Whenever I hear young people saying, "I want to be
somebody," I sometimes think of that little story. I say,
Why be satisfied with just being somebody? Be everybody!
Why love just one or two people who are close to you?
Love all! Take the whole world as your home; make every
mountain and river your own; treat every child – white,
black, brown, rich, poor – as your very own, and live in
a way that will make their earth a better place. That is the
real meaning of worship.

Coleridge put it well in his beautiful lines:

> He prayeth best who loveth best
> All things both great and small.
> For the dear God who loveth us,
> He made and loveth all.

Most of all, a trustee worships the universal spirit of life
by living up to his or her highest ideals. As soon as we begin
to live by our highest ideals, whether we consider ourselves
Christians or Jews or Moslems or Buddhists or simply

trustees of ourselves and the earth, all religious differences and quarrels disappear. In every sacred tradition, spiritual awareness means realizing the heart's deepest capacity for compassion, and that realization transcends all boundaries. If you live by the prayer of St. Francis of Assisi, not just repeating "Make me an instrument of peace" but actually trying to become an instrument of peace in your home, at your office, in your shop, or on your campus, nobody will ask what your religion is; no one will care. They will simply say, "I'm glad you're here. As long as there are people like you in the world, we have hope."

Becoming Zero

The tasks facing us today are enormous, but it is the glory of human nature that there will always be those rare individuals who say, "Let there be dangers, let there be difficulties, let there be the possibility of death itself – whatever it costs, I want to live to the full height of my being, with my feet still on the ground but my head crowned with stars." According to Mahatma Gandhi, this can be done only by facing difficulties that appear almost impossible. If that is so, the 1990s offer an unparalleled opportunity.

Our hope for the future lies with these rare evolutionaries who are not content to wait for others to change before they throw themselves into this unimaginably difficult task. "Strength of numbers is the delight of the timid," said Gandhi. "The valiant in spirit glory in fighting alone." These daring individuals simply laugh at the words "fun" and "pleasure." What is the satisfaction in drifting along with the current? True satisfaction lies in swimming against the current of conditioned self-interest. It is dangerous, of course, but that is why it makes you glow with vitality. It is strenuous, but that is what makes your will and determination and dedication grow strong, your senses clear, your mind secure, and your heart overflowing with love and the desire to give and serve.

Gandhi is a supreme example. He wanted so deeply to help the world that he dedicated his life to siphoning every trace of self-interest out of his heart and mind, leaving them pure, radiantly healthy, and free to love. It took him nearly twenty years to gain such control of his thinking process, but with every day of demanding effort he discovered a little more of the deep resources that are within us all: unassuming leadership, eloquence, and an endless capacity for selfless service.

When he was in South Africa, Gandhi sometimes would walk fifty miles in a day and sleep only a few hours a night. Even into his seventies he wrote hundreds of letters every week; when his right hand got tired, he learned to write with his left. Once, while he was writing a letter, the lantern failed. Most of us would have quit and gone to bed, but Gandhi, aware of how much his reply meant to those who had written him, went outside and finished his correspondence by moonlight. That kind of drive gives a glimpse of the wellspring of vitality he tapped every day. If we were asked to live like this, we would say, "Impossible!" Gandhi would object, "Oh, no. It *is* possible, when your mind is flooded with love for all."

How could anyone resist such a leader? His example inspired all of India to reach a little deeper for the perseverance, courage, and compassion we needed to carry on the struggle for independence. If a seventy-year-old man could work like that, how could we not follow his example?

Late in Gandhi's life a Western journalist asked, "Mr. Gandhi, you've been working fifteen hours a day for fifty years. Don't you ever feel like taking a few weeks off and going for a vacation?" Gandhi laughed and said, "Why? I am always on vacation." Because he had no personal irons in the fire, no selfish concerns involved in his work, there was no conflict in his mind to drain his energy. He had just one overwhelming desire – an ambition that, like a bonfire, had consumed all his passion. This world-famous figure, who could have been prime minister of India and one of the wealthiest men in Asia, declared he had no interest in becoming rich or famous. He wanted something far greater, he said: to become zero, to place all his talents, resources, time, and energy in a trust for the world.

In the climax of his great prayer, St. Francis proclaims, "It is in dying [to self] that we are born to eternal life." Although the media have been suggesting recently that self-sacrifice has gone out of fashion, I think there are still many young people – and older ones as well – who hunger for the adventure of such a challenge. It was not so long ago that John F. Kennedy said, "Ask not what your country can do for you; ask what you can do for your country," and millions of young people caught a tantalizing glimpse of a life based not on the feverish pursuit of personal profit, but on the exhilarating pursuit of a lofty, selfless goal.

Today, as we enter perhaps the most important and challenging decade in the history of mankind, it is only this irresistible, all-pervasive power locked away in our hearts that can guide us safely into the next millennium. "There comes a time," Gandhi wrote, "when an individual becomes irresistible and his action becomes all-pervasive in its effect. This comes when he reduces himself to zero." Let us ask not what life can give us, or how the earth can make a profit for us, or what corporations or governments can do for us. Let us each ask ourselves: How much can I give? How much can I love? How much can I remake my life?

Ultimately, in every one of the crises we are facing, the solution depends upon you and me. When we sit down to meditate in the morning, we are not just remaking our-selves. We are remaking our families, our community, our nation, and, in the end, our entire world.

In this great task, no one is unemployed. The Gita would say that all of us are given a job the moment we are born: our job is to give. Give till it hurts – and then give more. When it hurts more, give more.

Without the compassion, awareness, and wisdom hidden in each of our hearts, the world simply may not survive. The time has come when one by one we must learn to light the lamp of freedom and compassion within. Slowly, but very surely, the night will be filled with glowing lamps. There is no one else to do this job for us, and there may as yet be only a few of us who are ready to do it. But, as Emer-son put it, "when it is dark enough you can see the stars."

And once you've lit the lamp, keep it burning. "Full effort is full victory," said Gandhi. You need not be troubled if you have made mistakes, or if your ideal has slipped away. Just continue to give your best. If you fall, pick yourself up and march on. If you cannot run, walk. If you cannot walk, crawl. Nothing in life is more joyful or more thrilling. The effort alone brings a continuing wave of joy in which every personal problem, every suffering and humiliation, is forgotten.

Most of all, I believe, it is the young people of the world – especially in the developed countries, where we have the time and leisure to look inward – who can change the world's dangerous course. I have lived in the world of students for over fifty years, and the idealism I see in them gives me great hope for the future. Young people standing on the threshold of life always feel as if they are the first to discover the beauty of the world, and their love for that beauty can carry them to great heights.

I often used to teach Wordsworth to my college students in India, and I enjoyed seeing them nod in recognition at his marvelous lines:

> There was a time when meadow, grove, and stream,
> The earth, and every common sight,
> To me did seem
> Apparelled in celestial light,
> The glory and the freshness of a dream.

For those students, who were just beginning to hold up their own ideals like a lamp to the world, that vision must have seemed near enough to reach out and touch. I am sure they thought its glory and freshness would last forever. Yet, in the years that followed, when I chanced to meet up with some of them, it almost broke my heart to see how their ideals had been swept away by life's relentless tide of cares and pleasures. Gradually, many had become insensitive to the needs of the world around them. Because they had not learned how to keep the flame alive, they found themselves, as Wordsworth did, remembering the dreamy days of idealism from afar:

> It is not now as it hath been of yore; –
> Turn wheresoe'er I may,
> By night or day,
> The things which I have seen I now can see no more.

If there is one thing I would say to the young people of the world, it is this: don't ever lose your ideals. Time has a subtle way of stealing them when you least expect it. That night in Maritzburg, a small flame was lit in Gandhi's heart. It would have been very easy to let it be blown out – in a day, or a week, or even ten years. If he had let his ideal slip away, what would he have achieved? Nothing matters so much as keeping the flame alive. You can lose your hair, and nothing of significance is lost; you can lose your money, and nothing is lost; but if you lose your idealism, *you* are lost.

Yet for all of us there is hope. I know from my own experience that it is possible to rekindle that flame, even after the rough winds of life have reduced it to a flicker. It is possible, by the light of that ideal, to make a significant contribution to the health of the world. And it is possible, by that same light, to see the exquisite beauty of this compassionate universe.

As I have mentioned, it was while I was teaching at a great university in India that I took to meditation – with a passion that soon consumed all my other desires and aspirations. When I saw that it might be possible for an ordinary man like me to reach for that high ideal and live in its light always, I could not rest without it.

Many mystics have compared the gradual awakening of spiritual awareness to an approaching dawn. If you take up this great adventure of meditation, I am sure you too will come to know what it is like to look into a dark sky and see the first glimmers of a light you thought you would never see again, to hear the birds begin to sing, to feel the kind of intoxicating joy that overwhelmed me when I first saw the gates opening for a fuller, richer, deeper, harder life, dedicated to the service of my highest ideals – not in heaven but right here on earth.

I was particularly fond of poetry in those days, and I had a passion for the beauty of nature. Every summer, when the university was on vacation, I went to stay with my mother at our little bungalow on the Blue Mountain, high above the hot, dusty plains and far from the hectic rounds of academic life. At that point in my life, I would have assured you that I knew what beauty was; I drank from its wellsprings every day. But as my meditation deepened, I was amazed to find a new world opening up before me. At times it seemed that every tree I looked at had leaves that shone; every stream rushing down the hillside glittered with a brilliant light I had not seen in all my poetic observation. The birds' songs had become so beautiful that I felt I was hearing them not just with my ears but with my whole being. I remember thinking to myself, where have these wonderful birds come from?

In particular, I recall one day when I had just arrived for the summer, and saw the two jacaranda trees that stood in front of our home. I had seen them often, of course. They bloomed each year in mid-April, and my mother always said it was because her boy was coming home. But that day their blossoms were transfigured. In the early morning light they sparkled like so many vibrant jewels.

Suddenly I realized that what had changed was not outside in the trees and streams and birds, but inside me. As the mystics say, I was seeing the world by the light within. Through years of dedicated endeavor, the lamp had been lit in the depths of my consciousness, and all of nature had assumed an indescribable splendor. I recalled another stanza of Wordsworth's poignant poem – lines that evoke all the beauty of this compassionate universe and all the tragedy of lost ideals. When I had taught that poem to my students only a few months before, I had not understood what I was teaching:

> The rainbow comes and goes,
> And lovely is the rose;
> The moon doth with delight
> Look round her when the heavens are bare,
> Waters on a starry night
> Are beautiful and fair;
> The sunshine is a glorious birth;
> But yet I know, where'er I go
> That there hath past away a glory from the earth.

That morning on the Blue Mountain, I understood. Through my grandmother's grace, I had recaptured that glory, and it would never leave me. From the jacaranda blossoms on the Blue Mountain to the birds and seals on the farthest shore of the Pacific Ocean, the entire world had been placed in my hands. It was mine to love, to protect, and then to pass on – a little greener and more peaceful than I had found it – to another generation.

May you too recapture that glory – it belongs to you as it belongs to every human being – and may you light the world with it.

Notes

Chapter One

p. 17–19 Gandhi's life continues to be a source of inspiration for me. My book *Gandhi the Man* describes the transformation of this shy, ineffectual lawyer into the greatest force for peace in our times. Louis Fischer's *The Life of Mahatma Gandhi*, first published in 1950, is still an excellent resource; I have drawn on it for background on the Salt March described in Chapter Two. And finally, *An Autobiography: The Story of My Experiments With Truth*, written during the late twenties, describes Gandhi's life up to that point in his own words, with an honesty and simplicity which makes it unique among autobiographies. Most quotations from Gandhi in this book are drawn from these three sources.

Eknath Easwaran, *Gandhi the Man* (Petaluma, California: Nilgiri Press, 1978).

Louis Fischer, 1950 *The Life of Mahatma Gandhi* (New York: Harper & Row, Harper Colophon Books, 1983).

Mohandas K. Gandhi, *An Autobiography: the Story of My Experiments With Truth* (Boston: Beacon Press, 1957).

Chapter Two

p. 27–28 These comments on the secrets of advertising refer to a series of articles by Jonathan Rowe, "Modern Advertising: The Subtle Persuasion," in the Christian Science Monitor, January 27–29, 1987.

p. 30 Richard J. Barnet, *The Lean Years: Politics in the Age of Scarcity* (New York: Simon and Schuster, Touchstone ed., 1981), 23.

p. 32 "forced consumption" Victor Lebow quoted in *Blueprint for a Green Planet: Your Practical Guide to Restoring the World's Environment* John Seymour and Herbert Girardet (New York: Prentice Hall, 1987), 77.

p.33ff. For a thorough discussion of the problems inherent in the dependence on genetically engineered seed by agribusiness, see Jack Doyle's *Altered Harvest: Agriculture, Genetics, and the Fate of the World's Food Supply* (New York: Penguin Books, 1986).

p.36 "topsoil" *State of the World 1988* (New York: W.W. Norton & Company, 1988), 5. These annual reports by the Worldwatch Institute "on progress towards a sustainable society" are excellent resources for monitoring "the earth's vital signs." Each issue briefly updates the previous one and focuses on a handful of particular problems in thoroughly researched individual essays.

p.37 Barry Commoner in Wendell Berry, *The Unsettling of America* (New York: Avon, 1978), 198.

p.38 Thomas Berry, *The Dream of the Earth* (San Francisco: Sierra Club Books, 1988), 7.

p. 39–40 "extinction of species" Roger Lewin, "A Mass Extinction Without Asteroids," *Science* 234 (3 October 1986): 14–15. For a more extensive treatment see *The Last Extinction*, ed. Les Kaufman and Kenneth Mallory (Cambridge, Mass.: The MIT Press, 1986).

Chapter Three

p. 45–46 *The Bhagavad Gita*, trans. Eknath Easwaran (Petaluma, California: Nilgiri Press, 1985).

p. 46–47 W.I.B. Beveridge, *The Art of Scientific Investigation*, 3rd ed. (New York: Vintage Books, [1957]), 63.

p. 53 Paul Colinvaux in Robert Augros and George Stanciu's *The New Biology: Discovering the Wisdom in Nature* (Boston: Shambala, New Science Library, 1987), 99.

p. 53 Ibid., Frits Went, 93–94.

p. 55 Edward O. Wilson, as reported by Roger Lewin, "Damage to Tropical Forests, or Why Were There So Many Kinds of Animals?," *Science* 234 (10 October 1986): 149–50.

p. 55 The plight of the world's rainforests first struck me on my visits to my home in Kerala, South India, but since then their destruction has become a global concern. For this section I have consulted Catherine Caufield's *In the Rainforest: Report from a Strange, Beautiful, Imperiled World* (Chicago: University of Chicago Press, 1986), and numerous updates in the popular press.

p. 56 "songbirds" Jack Connor, "Empty Skies: Where Have All the Songbirds Gone?," *Harrowsmith* 3:16 (July/August 1988): 34 and Paul Ehrlich's article, "Winged Warning," *Sierra* 73:5 (September/October 1988): 57.

p. 56 "Greenhouse effect" On June 23, 1988, NASA climatologist Dr. James Hansen went before a congressional committee and declared that he was "99% certain. . . that the greenhouse is here." It made front pages all over the country, and for weeks it was the lead story in the popular press. (Newsweek, June 11, 1988). By fall, local papers were reporting on the dire effects predicted for their particular area. Most news journals report on new research and legislation as it occurs. See also Worldwatch's *State of the World* each year. For a recent scientific update, see Richard A. Houghton and George M. Woodwell, "Global Climatic Change," *Scientific American* 260:4 (April 1989): 36.

p.58 Barry Commoner, *The Closing Circle: Nature, Man & Technology* (New York: Bantam, 1972), 42.

p.59 John Eddy quoted by James R. Udall in "Turning Down the Heat," *Sierra* 74:4 (July/August 1989): 29.

p.61–64 "CFCs" For a brief, readable account of the development of CFCs and the discovery of their effects on the ozone layer, see Robert H. Boyle's "Forecast for Disaster," *Sports Illustrated* 67:21 (November 16, 1987): 79. For proposals to remedy the situation, see Cynthia Pollock Shea, "Protecting the Ozone Layer," in *State of the World 1989*, p. 77.

p.64–65 Michael Oppenheimer quoted in "Forecast for Disaster," p.90.

Chapter Four

p.75 "minimum consumption" E.F. Schumacher, 1973, *Small is Beautiful: Economics as if People Mattered* (New York: Harper & Row, Perennial Library ed.1975), 57.

p.75 "cultivation of needs" Ibid., 33.

p.76 Barry Commoner, *The Closing Circle*, 37.

p.81–82 J.C. Kumarappa quoted in Schumacher's *Small is Beautiful*, 56.

Chapter Five

p.85 Schumacher, *Small is Beautiful,* 61.

p.86 "ordinary people" Thomas A. Sancton, "Planet of the Year," *Time* 133:1 (January 2, 1989): 30.

p.89 "sustainable economics" William U. Chandler, "Designing Sustainable Economies," in Worldwatch Institute's *State of the World 1987* (New York: W.W. Norton & Company, 1987), 177.

p.90–93 "waste" The garbage problem appears regularly in the news, especially as a local issue, though some cities have tried to solve it by shipping it overseas. For a useful overview of the problem, see Cynthia Pollock's "Realizing Recycling's Potential" in *State of the World 1987,* p. 101.

p.94 "CO2 emissions" James R. Udall "Domestic Calculations," *Sierra* 74:4 (July/August 1989): 33.

p.95 "trees" James R. Udall, "Turning Down the Heat," *Sierra* 74:4 (July/August 1989): 32.

p.103 Beveridge, *The Art of Scientific Investigation,* 66.

Chapter Six

p.112 Eknath Easwaran, *Meditation* (Petaluma, California: Nilgiri Press, 1978).

p.128 *The New Laurel's Kitchen* (Berkeley, California: Ten Speed Press, 1986) is the second edition of this classic cookbook. My friends Laurel Robertson, Carol Flinders, and Brian Ruppenthal have seen to it that it reflects the latest in nutritional knowledge as well as the best cooking we know – good for us and good for the earth.

Chapter Seven

p.152 "the power of love" Martin Luther King, Jr., *A Testament of Hope: the Essential Writings of Martin Luther King Jr.* ed. James Melvin Washington (San Francisco: Harper & Row, 1986) 38.

p.152 "Gandhi and the love ethic" Martin Luther King, Jr. *Stride Towards Freedom: The Montgomery Story* (New York: Harper & Row, 1958), 97.

p.152–53 "I've seen too much hate. . . " Martin Luther King, Jr. *Testament,* p.256–257.

p.153 "the common enemy" James R. Udall "Turning Down the Heat," 32.

Chapter Eight

p.158 Thomas Lovejoy, quoted in *State of the World 1989,* p. 192. A biologist, Lovejoy is Assistant Secretary for External Affairs of the Smithsonian Institution.

p.170 William Wordsworth, "Ode: Intimations of Immortality from Recollections of Early Childhood" in *William Wordsworth, Selected Poems and Prefaces* ed. Jack Stillinger (Boston: Houghton Mifflin, Riverside ed., 1965), 186.

Index

Easwaran, Eknath.

    The compassionate universe / by Eknath Easwaran.

      p.   cm.

    ISBN 0–915132–59–1 : $22.00.

    ISBN 0–915132–58–3 (pbk.) : $12.00

    1. Human ecology – Moral and ethical aspects.

2. Nature – Religious aspects. 3. Philosophy of nature. I. Title.

GF80.E18 1989

304.2 – dc20   89–23058

                           CIP